Praise for

Wild Ideas: Creativity from the Inside Out

······ˑ··●

"What an accomplishment . . . COURAGEOUS, INTIMATE, SOULFUL, INSIGHTFUL! I feel grateful to have found *Wild Ideas*."

—JUDY ABBATE, AWARD-WINNING GRAPHIC DESIGNER

"Cathy Wild is a creative spirit who has written a brave exploration of her personal journey interwoven with wise, encouraging guidance and beautifully chosen quotes. If you long to be a creator, *Wild Ideas* will support you in discovering and following the voice of your soul."

—KAYLEEN ASBO, PH.D., CULTURAL HISTORIAN, MUSICIAN, WRITER, AND FACULTY AT THE SAN FRANCISCO CONSERVATORY OF MUSIC

"An intimate, authentic look at creativity. Cathy really did her homework. As a working artist, I had many moments of validation for my own process. *Wild Ideas* is a great tool for those interested in their own creative journey."

—CHRIS HENRY, FINE ARTIST AND TEACHER

"Cathy is a wonderful storyteller and teacher. *Wild Ideas* is so full of heart—and for me, very experiential. As I connect with Cathy's stories, I can *feel* the visceral impact of her wisdom teachings. *Wild Ideas* shines a much-needed light into the mysteries of the creative process."

—DIANNE NEUMANN, MFCC, FINE ARTIST AND TEACHER

"More than a beautifully written book, *Wild Ideas* is a toolkit for anyone wanting to work and think outside the box—it's not just for artists. Cathy's insights inspired me to expand the limits of my conventional thinking about an important case so I could develop an innovative strategy on behalf of a client."

—STEPHEN SILVERMAN, STEPHEN SILVERMAN LAW

"Reading Cathy's brave, insightful book was a life-changing experience for me. I now understand that my deepest secrets, secrets I used to hide, can be a source of creative power."

—GUY CONNER, POLITICAL CONSULTANT

"It's been years since I found myself sneaking off in the middle of the day to read a book . . . the only other book about the creative process that drew me in this way was *Bird By Bird* by Anne Lamott."

—DEBBIE GRAY, GRAPHIC DESIGNER

"As an artist I have read many books on creativity. This is the first one that resonated with my mind, heart, and soul at a level that unleashed my personal power. I found something of value on every page."

—ELAINE LARSEN, ARTIST AND REIKI MASTER

"Full of warmth and wisdom, Cathy's engaging and compassionate approach to the creative process helped me rekindle passions I had long since abandoned. I felt inspired to believe in myself. *Wild Ideas: Creativity from the Inside Out* may well become the most well-worn book in my personal library."

—JOEL CROCKETT, OWNER, FOUR-EYED FROG BOOKS

"I have so many ideas but I never get very far with them. Reading *Wild Ideas* moved me to get started on an important project I'd been putting off for years."

—LISA HAYDON, M.S.ED., OTR, DOMINICAN UNIVERSITY OF CALIFORNIA

"I wish I'd had *Wild Ideas: Creativity from the Inside Out* thirty years ago, when I wanted to get back to the creative being I was as a child, when my favorite pastime was to draw. There is a section for everyone, no matter where you are along the creative path. I will buy this book for my friends. I will keep it by my bed as a testament to my creative possibilities."

—AUDREY VON HAWLEY, SONOMA COLLAGE STUDIO

"Cathy Wild provides a wonderful resource for anyone at any age on their creative journey. Drawing from her own rich experience, honestly and with great depth of understanding and compassion, Cathy has created an eloquent guide and companion that covers every aspect of the creative process. I would recommend *Wild Ideas* to anyone seeking greater clarity and encouragement on the path to creative fulfillment."

—BARBARA JACOBSEN, SONOMA TREASURE ARTIST

"*Wild Ideas* explores vital aspects of the creative process interwoven with the author's own deeply personal journey to realize her creative ambitions. Like the iconic *Zen and the Art of Motorcycle Maintenance* or *Adventures in the Screen Trade,* this thought-provoking book has the power to inspire and move readers along their own path to a more fulfilling creative life."

—RAY DEAN MIZE, AWARD-WINNING SHORT STORY, TELEVISION, AND FILM WRITER

WILD IDEAS

Creativity from the Inside Out

WILD IDEAS

Creativity from the Inside Out

Cathy Wild

STANDING PLACE PRESS
SANTA ROSA, CALIFORNIA

Standing Place Press
1275 Fourth Street #386
Santa Rosa, CA 95404
Phone: 707.540.5948
Email: cathy@cathywild.com
Website: cathywild.com

Cover Artwork and Art Direction: Cathy Wild
Design: Bostian Design
Back Cover Photo: Barbara McChesney

Author's Note: The names of friends and clients mentioned in *Wild Ideas: Creativity from the Inside Out* have been changed to protect their privacy. The stories, scenes, and dialogue are recounted to the best of my recollection. Certain vignettes have been combined from several people to illustrate key points and further protect confidentiality. You may see yourself in these pages because I am writing about universal human experiences. Additionally, this book is meant to inform and inspire readers on their creative journeys. It is not intended as a prescriptive solution for problems with addiction or other chronic or severe psychological illness such as clinical depression or bipolar disorder. Please seek professional assistance from your local mental health professional or agency.

Ordering Information: Special discounts are available on quantity purchases. For details contact "Special Sales Department" at the address above.

ISBN: 978-0-9968105-0-0
Printed in the USA
Library of Congress Control Number: 2016943736
First edition

for my mother,

june field

(lost dreamer, creative soul)

If you have the vision and urge

to undertake great tasks,

then you will discover in yourself the virtues

and the capabilities required for their accomplishment.

—*Henry Miller*

CONTENTS

[This book] is sent out to those into whose souls
the iron of adversity has entered, and has entered deeply
at some time in their lives . . .

—*Thomas Hardy*

Creativity emerges from the inner yearning
to find and express meaning in life.

—Judith Gomez

Become aware of what is in you. Announce it,
pronounce it, produce it, and give birth to it.

—Meister Eckhart

Time swiftly passes by and opportunity is lost. Each
of us should strive to awaken. Awaken. Take heed.
Do not squander your life.

—Dogen Zenji (1200–1253)

Opening
to the reader

THE FINISH LINE WAS IN SIGHT but I couldn't bring myself to cross it. After years of hard work, all the joy and passion I'd been pouring into these pages just seemed to dry up. I had hit another wall, another impasse in which I was questioning everything, including my sanity. What was it all for anyway? My greatest fear seemed to be coming to pass: I didn't have enough of whatever it took to finish this book, and I didn't have the energy to care.

It was definitely time for a break. I decided to step back from the project for a while to gain some badly needed perspective. There were, after all, other things going on in the world. Amazingly enough, some people seemed perfectly capable of finding meaning in their lives without needing to wake up every day and write—I had an overpowering urge to go out and find them.

About a month later, I went searching for inspiration in San Miguel d'Allende, a cultural oasis nestled in the high desert mountains north of Mexico City. I spent time wandering the narrow streets, poking around colorful marketplaces, soaking in the nearby hot springs, and luxuriating in long walks and even longer conversations with my friend Cheryl, an old friend from high school who agreed to join me for a few days.

One particularly memorable exchange took place as we were walking in the hills around town. We were just coming up to an expanse with a breathtaking view. The sky beyond was ablaze with a glorious crimson sunset. Cheryl and I stood side by side, silently taking it all in, when she suddenly remarked, "I just want to wake up in the morning and sink my teeth into something that makes my soul sing."

At once, time seemed to stop as my friend's words lit up, all electric, like a neon sign pointing the way to my heart. And right there, in that magical moment, I remembered why I had been sitting alone in front of my computer day after day. I had been attempting to answer that longing with this book.

It is my hope that some of my own hard-won wisdom can be shared with others who, like myself, hunger for a life that is creatively focused—a life that is engaged, purposeful, and fulfilled. A life that sings.

·····..·..●

Many of us long to express ourselves in some way that awakens our unquestionable and vibrant connection to life. We hunger for something more—just like my friend Cheryl, who eventually found her passion. About a year after our splendid sojourn, Cheryl took an extended sabbatical and actually moved to San Miguel. Blossoming in the vibrancy of her new surroundings, she completed her first novel. My friend Sam had a similar breakthrough. He gave up a lucrative screenwriting career in Hollywood to become a high school teacher in the examples to your particular situation. Honor your own rhythms.

Although *Wild Ideas* is not a "how-to" workbook full of creativity exercises, I have included questions in each section to encourage you to reflect about what you are reading and help you apply it to your own process. I suggest that you work deeply with only a few questions at a time. Give your body, mind, and spirit enough time and space for wholehearted contemplation so that your natural impulses toward healing, inspiration, and creative possibility can find you.

Remember, the questions are opportunities for exploration, not assignments. You can write, draw, dance, paint, or meditate on a single question. Don't press yourself for definitive answers; *Wild Ideas* isn't a test. In this case, *guessing* will almost always yield a valuable result. You might try reading a question just before drifting off to sleep. Over the next few days a response may float up in the form of a subtle sensation, suggestion, or fleeting thought. Reflecting on your own process catalyzes awareness and wisdom, empowering you to ask honest questions. The more open and honest you are, the more notes you make, the more likely you will turn reflection into action.

······•

Wild Ideas is grounded in extensive research and my own creative recovery, as well as more than thirty years of process-work with clients. Writing *Wild Ideas* has been as much a journey of personal discovery for me as reading this book will be for you. I set out to write an honest and passionate account of the creative journey from the inside out. Somewhere along the way, I realized that my own experience while birthing this book was integral to the story.

I often write from a sense of personal authority and wisdom about the creative process. But I also write to explore what I think, what I feel, and what my experience means. I most resonate with writing that expresses the rawness of being human. If I succeed in connecting with you, it will be because you can see and feel much of my own process. I have been to the darkest depths of creative doubt and frustration and found my way back to the light. I hope that what you will find in these pages is an informative and compassionate look into the joys and challenges of creativity as it applies to both art and life.

All creators struggle to find their own road—whether they are writers, carpenters, sculptors, scientists, entrepreneurs, athletes, parents, composers, or chefs. Ideas have the power to expand our minds, open our hearts, and inspire us on our journey. May these *Wild Ideas* support you in coming home to your own innate creativity.

—Cathy Wild

You either walk inside your story

and own it

or you stand outside

and hustle for your worthiness.

—*Brené Brown*

*Where I create I am true, and I want to find the
strength to build my life wholly upon this truth,
upon this infinite simplicity and joy.*

—Rainer Maria Rilke

*We are all preparing for that abrupt waking and
that calling . . . that moment we have to say Yes!*

—David Whyte

*All life is an experiment. The more experiments
you make the better.*

—Mark Twain

My Journey
narrative truth

FOR AS LONG AS I CAN REMEMBER, I have admired creative people
and, for much of my life, never considered myself to be one of them.
I understood nothing about the creative process. Indeed, I didn't
even realize creativity involved any sort of "process." I just assumed
that creative people knew what to do and did it—effortlessly. I also
assumed that to be creative, you had to have a touch of genius or at
least, be blessed with a recognizable talent. As far as I was concerned,
that left me out completely.

"We teach what we need to learn" is an adage that certainly applies
to me . . .

Early on, my experiences in school pretty much nail the coffin
on my capacity for creative expression. In Mrs. Skinner's third-grade
class I am the only girl who does not get into the school chorus. I feel
so nervous singing in front of the teacher that all I can manage is a
humiliating squawk as my voice struggles to reach the high notes of

the requisite audition song, "America the Beautiful." After school lets out, I can't wait to get home so I can dump out my big box of Crayola Crayons. I select one of the slender shafts at random and draw free form designs—purely for the joy of experiencing color. Back at school, I discover that I have even less aptitude for art than I do for singing. I cannot draw a realistic image to save my life, and my meager attempts at crafts produce pathetic puddles of clay with curled edges—*ashtrays*—that I dutifully bring home to my mother, who smiles weakly and says nothing.

Each semester, my report card reminds me that I am not talented, therefore not creative. In my junior high sewing class, I actually get a D on my gym bag. Anyone can sew a gym bag; it's just a square of material with straight stitching on three sides. Anyone can—but apparently not me. How can I face my grandmother: a woman so supremely confident in her creative capacities that she could, over a weekend, design and whip out a fully lined coat complete with covered buttons? Shame overcomes me; I am a creative incompetent.

I eventually learn to lip-sync and to avoid any activity that requires me to use my hands. Still, I am drawn to the unconventional lives of creative people. My heroes are explorers, cowboys and cowgirls, blues singers, artists, and writers—smart, independent people who disregard social conventions and leave familiar places in order to journey into uncharted lands. I feel myself to be one of them in spirit, but I don't know how to live a life that expresses that spirit. Much of the time I am aware of a restless longing that drives me in search of something I cannot name . . .

·····ᐧ··•

After graduating from college, I try to find satisfying work in a number of fields—as a personal assistant, sound editor, script supervisor, health food store manager, cook, bartender, preschool teacher, alternative-school administrator, and more. But no matter what sort of job I have, I always feel so totally drained by the end of the day that I never manage to stick with it for more than a year. Eventually, I find the nine-to-five work environment so monotonous and dispiriting I just can't bear to be in the workforce. But I also can't think of doing anything else.

·······•

I am twenty-four when I finally give up, get married, and seek a hopeful refuge in the languorous beauty of a Caribbean island. Once the novel excitement of this latest adventure wears thin, I wake up one morning and discover, to my horror, the same gnawing restlessness has found me hiding in my watery idyll. As if to mock me, it reasserts itself with a stunning vengeance. There is nowhere to hide. My deep need for meaningful self-expression cannot be silenced and there is no escape from finding a means for its expression.

When my husband and I return from our expatriate experiment in paradise, we move back to Venice, a small Southern California beach community in the midst of a creative renaissance. In the 1970s, many artists and filmmakers move their studios into the cheap warehouse spaces. Pioneering young chefs open restaurants featuring locally sourced ingredients; artists adorn formerly abandoned buildings with colorful murals; and writers start hip, arty magazines. Rundown neighborhoods of classic beach bungalows bustle with the activity of restoration. It seems as if everyone I know is participating in this great resurgence except me. I watch from the sidelines with a mix of envy, frustration, admiration, and awe. How do they do it? And why can't I?

In desperation, I make one last attempt to break into "something exciting." I try to get a job as a publicist for a major movie studio.

A friend in the business introduces me to a man who had been her mentor. I think I have it made. After several interviews over lunch with wine, I wait for the phone call that will magically transform my life. But when it finally comes, he invites me to his home—his wife has left town for the weekend and we can discuss the job that evening. He finishes the conversation with a salacious reference to one of my body parts. When I hang up the phone, I burst into tears. I had been so lost in the stars I didn't even see it coming.

The incident proves to be a final and mortifying end to my attempts to find what I considered a real job in the nine-to-five world. I have hit bottom. My humiliating defeat forces me to do the one thing I have been avoiding my entire young life. I have to turn inward and dig deep into my inner resources—however thin I feel them to be. I will have to invent a job and a life. The well-worn paths that others have walked don't seem to work for me. I accept the challenge.

·······•

Paradoxically, when you have nothing left to lose and your existence seems most wretched—happily—you may be ripe for inspiration to find you. My breakthrough comes while browsing through a magazine. I chance upon a story about a former ballerina who teaches stretching classes in New York City. Some time after that I get the idea that changes my life.

I was naturally fit in high school, but in the years afterward, I battle sugar cravings while gaining and losing the same ten or fifteen pounds over and over. But even more dispiriting than the yo-yo weight struggles is the fact that I haven't really felt all that well for a long time. In an interesting synchronicity, I read the article about the ballerina just at the point when the focus of my life for the previous year has been on healing my body. I have recently gotten back into shape with a combination of whole foods, herbs—and an exercise program that I created myself. It is really working for me. I have never felt better in my life.

Because I tried and failed to find satisfaction in so many different work environments, I finally feel ready to try something completely different. "Why not!" I say to myself, when the thought of starting my own business begins rattling around in my mind. "I'm scared to death, but really, what else is there to do at this point?"

I decide to offer my program to people in the privacy of their homes and offices. That way, I haven't invested in overhead if things don't work out. I call my service "Body Conditioning." At this time, there aren't careers called "fitness trainer" or "wellness coach." The running craze is just starting to take off, some health clubs still offer vibrating equipment to eliminate fat, and Jane Fonda is still better known as an actress than as a health-and-fitness guru.

I don't have a clue about what I am doing. I just make it up as I go along, blindly following my instincts. But the Universe responds almost immediately to help me, once I commit to take the risk. I swear this is true: While driving over to my father's house for a family dinner, I practically careen into my former high-school boyfriend— now a writer for the *Los Angeles Times*—under a freeway overpass that borders the neighborhood. When I tell him about my new venture, he volunteers to introduce me to the editor at *Los Angeles Magazine*. The resulting sidebar interview that runs in the magazine launches my business. No, I don't become an overnight sensation—my real-life journey is a lot messier than a movie—but I do well enough to realize I should keep trusting my instincts. I have taken an important step, and from that point on, I never look back.

Strangely enough, it never occurs to me that what I am doing has any remote connection to the creative process. I don't realize that I am, in fact, a creative person—not simply a misplaced person—until many years later.

······ ··●

Eventually I find the confidence to leave my unhappy marriage and move to Northern California, and on to other ways of turning my intuitive gifts and interests into my livelihood—this time as a "Personal Development Consultant." Once again, there are no precedents for me to follow—the career of "life coaching" has not yet been invented.

By now I begin to experience a pervasive sense that I am being led. I have no religious or spiritual influences in my upbringing, so I have no way to understand my feelings. My father the scientist worships in the hallowed House of Rationality. All experience can be explained by physics and biology, and especially by the power of the intellect. Clearly, my experiences and insights are stretching me far beyond my father's view of the world. It begins to dawn on me that there might be unseen forces or energies in the universe. I am somehow tapping into them. Maybe if I can do this more intentionally, I can form a kind of *partnership with the Universe.* (I also spend quite a bit of time questioning my sanity during this period but, in the end, it seems too depressing not to give this more hopeful perspective a chance.)

More pieces fall into place. I begin to feel companioned by an inner excitement whose presence suggests I am living more authentically. I am definitely on a path; I am answering the call by doing whatever it takes to do the work I feel meant to do in this world; I am not fighting the sacrifices it requires anymore; and most importantly I am learning and growing. Yet something is still missing from my understanding—because even the act of successfully reinventing myself for a second time doesn't strike me as creative.

······ ··●

My research into the creative process begins with a decision to market seminar and speaking services to corporate clients. Ronald Reagan is president and business is cool again. I am looking for a different angle on the management consulting field. After interviewing a potential client, I sense that *creativity* is an area that might be of interest to them. I have no way of knowing that this research will change the course of my life.

I read books about the creative process like Rollo May's *The Courage to Create* and Willis Harman's *Higher Creativity*. After a lifetime of thrashing around in the dark, I am learning that the things creators do aren't so mysterious after all. Creativity can be broken down into a step-by-step process, and, more significantly, I see how my life fits into that process. I realize that all those years of experimentation and false starts corresponded to what Harman calls the *research* and *incubation* stages of the creative process. As more missing pieces fall into place, I no longer view the creative process as separate from the act of living my life: They are one and the same thing! I have been doing it all along!

In a eureka moment like nothing I had ever experienced, this new, holistic perspective completely changes my view of myself and my understanding of what it means to be creative. For the first time in my life, I acknowledge myself to be an artist. And it has nothing to do with art. I begin to see that music, paintings, and books emerge from a creator's willingness to experiment and explore ideas amidst intense feelings, especially negative ones. Frustration, anxiety, self-doubt, uncertainty, confusion—all the emotions I had judged as premonitions of failure—are part of the process. Most of all, the skills required to pursue that process have more to do with passion and persistence than with talent.

Passion, I have. And strengthening my capacity for persistence is definitely doable. Finally I have a map for navigating the world that makes sense to me—and a path to achieve my secret longing to be an artist.

This breakthrough unleashes an explosion of creative energy.

The years I spend researching creativity and conducting creativity workshops so radically transforms my own relationship to the vicissitudes of the creative process that I stop teaching altogether. I start writing and making art instead. The quarterly publication I create eventually becomes a column that appears online and in a number of local papers. Researchers at PBS find one of my articles and ask me to appear in a television special about creativity in midlife. I also have several art shows and am fortunate enough to sell many of my pieces. However, the satisfaction of overcoming so many internal obstacles to personal expression and fulfillment, while helping others heal and thrive, proves to be the most enduring source of emotional and spiritual sustenance.

Today, I am discovering new levels of strength and courage as the creative process continues to draw me into uncharted territory, revealing new vistas that at once beckon and terrify. I have never been faced so often with the truth of my own inadequacies, fears, and doubts. When these emotional challenges threaten to overwhelm my faith in myself, I take solace in remembering something my father wrote to me on my fortieth birthday: "When you are no longer surprised, exhilarated, or threatened by what happens—it's over. Take time to enjoy your accomplishments and anticipated pleasures."

All creative paths lead both inside and outside.

—*Stephen Mitchell*

I paint in order not to cry.

—Paul Klee

Who is it that can tell me who I am?

—Shakespeare, King Lear

The world breaks everyone and afterward,
some are strong at the broken places.

—Ernest Hemingway

My Journey
emotional truth

I BELIEVE WITH ALL MY HEART that creativity is the natural state of each
of us. It is our birthright. We are born with an instinct to express
ourselves, just as we are born with an instinct to survive. We come into
this world whole and connected to our capacity to give voice to our
feelings and desires.

But something happens to us in the process of growing up that
disconnects us from that voice. Early in life, many of us become
wounded. If we don't have the resources to deal with this psychic
pain, we split away from the part of ourselves that is hurting. In the
process, we lose trust in our ourselves and our most basic instincts.
Indeed, we actually begin to fear—or even hate—this *shadow self*.
We construct a variety of elaborate defenses against it. As a result, we
lose the capacity to hear our inner promptings. We begin to believe
that we have nothing original or valuable to offer. Our lives become
rote—prescribed by the expectations of others. Often, we don't even

realize that we are living the life someone else wants for us until we are well into our middle years.

Sometimes this forgotten part of ourselves expresses its frustrations quietly, as a faint dissatisfaction or malaise; at other times, frustration may build to a boiling point, becoming disruptive and destructive to ourselves or others. The untapped energy of the *shadow self* frequently seeks an outlet through the body, presenting as physical and/or psychological symptoms. Some of us have a strong instinct to repair this split and we become "seekers." In an attempt to reunite with our abandoned self, we are searching for a way to make ourselves whole. The creative process is a way to facilitate this quest.

······ · ··•

The loss of my mother sets me up for my long and painful journey. Not long after my birth, my mother becomes overwhelmed by the demands of caring for a helpless infant on her own. With my father spending long hours at the hospital as part of his medical training— coming home exhausted, in need of nurturing himself—my mother starts using prescription drugs and eventually alcohol to numb whatever demons are overwhelming her capacity to cope.

By the time my sister is born, my mother can barely get out of bed each day. She sees psychiatrists who prescribe more and more medication. She tries psychoanalysis and then shock therapy—but nothing really works for long. My early life is characterized by hope after failed hope until one day, my mother passes out in bed with a burning cigarette and the house goes up in flames around her.

HOME Scary Unpredictable Heavy No Adults Know what to Do about Mother or the terrible Pain we are all suffering. Passive disquiet erupts into

Violent outbursts of Rage and Blame. There's a lot of yelling and crying and silence. >>Home is an emotional Battle Ground<< Each person struggles to survive a problem that has no name. There is no fix. It is the 1950s. No one speaks out loud about such terrible suffering. No one Confesses. No one is Redeemed or Saved.

······ᐧ··●

Alerted by the smell of smoke, our neighbor breaks a window and pulls my mother to safety. (OK, saved but not SAVED, not in the way that I meant.)

Hospitalized for weeks, she finally comes home to our rented apartment to convalesce . . . and much later . . . we all move back to our refurbished house. We all want to believe that this will be a new beginning. We hug. We laugh. We sing. She makes sour cream pancakes for breakfast and remembers to pack my lunch.

it is a Frail Happiness; still, we need to believe in it for a little while . . .

because too soon it all starts again. She stays in bed most of the day. She forgets to pick us up at school. There is never enough food, enough love, enough light, enough life . . . Enough? . . . there is never enough in our house.

One night, my father finds a cigarette burn in the reupholstered couch. Enraged. Despondent. He finally does the unthinkable . . .

The men that come for her are dressed in white coats, "like the milkman," I whisper to my little sister.

I am too embarrassed to tell anyone. My mother never returns home. Life is less scary once she is gone. I don't want to see her again for a long, l o n g time.

······•

I miss (having a mother but I don't miss) my mother.

······•

Part of me grows up lost, insecure, and ashamed. I whirl in a motherless vortex. There are so many gaps in my development; I am constantly struggling to catch up. When I can't fill in the gaps, I try to hide what feel like huge defects in my being so I can appear as normal as possible.

<<*A Memory*>> *I am looking at myself in a mirror to see if the holes in my body are showing.*

······•

Another part of me, miraculously, finds a way to thrive amidst neglect. My imagination flourishes in the perverse freedom abandonment affords me. I spend hours away from home—riding my bike, playing in the streets, and reading in the library. All the girls are reading stories about horses, but not me. I devour real-life tales of adventure detailing the exploits of explorers and pioneers who left home in search of something else. Their daring, courageous lives inspire hope. I don't know how yet, but—one day—I will change my life too.

I channel my inconsolable heartbreak and isolation into a passion to live an authentic and completely original life. On one level I live fearless and determined . . . on another, I am broken. But it will be many years before I consciously know about that.

······•

A naturally talented dancer and singer, my mother never found the courage, confidence, or discipline to focus and express her talents effectively. I grew up terrified that her tragic fate would become my own. Where she had failed, I felt compelled to succeed. Where she was weak, I would be strong. I swore to discover my gifts and use them wisely and well. My existence needed to count for something.

By necessity, I was drawn to understand and explore the dark and forbidding corners of my psyche; and that journey has been my best teacher. What my mother was unable to do for herself, I learned to do. I grew in my self-understanding; I learned to use the dynamic tension between the pull of fear and push of passion; I forgave the pain. I forgave my mother. . . . I forgave my father. . . . I forgave the doctors. . . . And I forgave myself for not being able to save her.

Then I began to share what I learned from the inside out with others.

My mother has been my greatest source of heartbreak as well as my inspiration. Ultimately, the creative process can help us find meaning and purpose in pain. When we create, we can elevate and transform longing and loss into something that inspires others, healing ourselves in the process.

Although I really had no idea exactly where I was headed, my quest eventually led me to express myself as a teacher, healer, artist, and writer. *Where will your adventure take you?* It begins when you consider the compelling questions that inform the creative journey.

What do I want from life?

What do I long to express?

What gifts or personal qualities can I share with the world?

Where can I stand within myself in order to find the love, the strength, and the resources?

What do I need to heal in order to begin?

*There's something in us that strives, that aspires to
bring things into being that didn't exist before.*

—Robert Fritz

*In order to create there must be a dynamic force, and
what force is more potent than love?*

—Igor Stravinsky

*There is a vitality, a life force, an energy, a
quickening that is translated through you . . .*

—Martha Graham

1
Feeling
Inspired

A VOICE OF INSPIRATION inside each of us struggles to be heard.
Sometimes this voice speaks with agitated insistence. At
other times its urgings murmur like a soft breeze we barely
notice: a fleeting image, an elusive idea, a subtle longing that dissipates
before it can even be named. Whether subjected to shouts or whispers,
some of us spend years refusing the call because to acknowledge it
demands changes that seem frightening or impossibly complex.

The anxiety associated with creative expression frequently prevents
us from taking even this first step of acknowledgement. We remain
crippled by doubt, rendered mute by feelings of unworthiness, or
immobilized by expectations of failure.

Yet there is something else inside. That still, small voice you've been
ignoring actually possesses more strength than all your fears: *Wake up*, it
implores. *Take a chance!* As scary as it sometimes feels, you can trust its
power to lead you home.

Inner critic –
CaTrolley
Frolly

vs.

Denali
Lolly

In choosing to answer the call, we initiate an act of love. For it is love that moves us to respond, that gives us the strength to overcome our doubts and fears. And it is love that inspires us to grow beyond our limited perceptions of ourselves.

Some liken the voice of inspiration to a summons from the Divine Mystery itself. Whatever its ultimate source, the call is an invitation to relationship—a hope for something greater, fuller, and more meaningful. Much will be asked of you—not only to *do* something new, but to *be* something new as well—but much will be given in return.

If you have been ignoring or running from your inner promptings, perhaps you can now no longer dismiss what longs to express itself through you. *Perhaps you are ready to answer.*

Once you acknowledge the call to create and are moved to respond, you have begun a dialogue with your feelings of inspiration: *Hello. What do you want?*

Although the connection is tentative at first, a channel has been opened, a mutual relationship initiated. You are no longer alone. The dynamic that will move you through all the stages of the creative process begins here, in the encounter with inspiration. This connection is filled with alternating currents of excitement and anxiety—producing the emotional energy you need to act, fueling the quest to completion.

Whether this spark ignites a creative fire depends on how well you nurture the qualities from which all acts of creative inspiration spring: *desire, imagination, purpose, curiosity,* and *risk.*

Desire drives the heart's hunger for connection and self-expression. *Imagination* visualizes what the heart longs for. *Purpose* grounds and purifies the heart's desire. *Curiosity* opens the mind and engages the unknown. *Risk* dares action, takes chances—and makes the creative journey possible.

A strong passion for any objective will ensure success,
for the desire of the end will point out the means.

—William Hazlitt

Let yourself be silently drawn by the stronger pull of
what you really love.

—Rumi

So don't ask yourself what people want. Ask instead,
what is true? What really inspires me, excites me?

—David Edwards

Desire

THE JUICY, EXCITED FEELING of desire keeps life in motion. Has the
luster of your current lifestyle lost its glow? Have you ever wondered
what it would be like to leave that high-stress job you've held for
twenty years and move to Panama to open a bed & breakfast? Have
you fantasized about turning a weed-infested lot into a community
garden? Or do you long to go back to school and study painting—or
write your first book at the age of sixty-five? . . . Desire is the impulse
that sparks the flame.

Without desire, our existence becomes remote and passionless. We
need the energy of desire to come alive—but not all desires are created
equal. Some desires propel us toward satisfying self-expression, connection, and service. Others entice and titillate, leaving us lost in a parade
of empty distractions, as one desire spirals endlessly into another.

Consumer culture tends to amplify our superficial and incidental desires so much that we can't hear our deeper longings. How then do we distinguish *genuine* desire from *distorted* desire? How do we tell the difference between the internal urgency that signals empty obsession and the deep need that compels us toward authenticity?

······ ··●

True desire comes from the heart. It speaks to some deeper and more meaningful truth. *What do I care about? What really matters?* These questions call us home to ourselves. Once our dreams slip into shadow, they can become obscured or distorted by empty preoccupations. In such cases, it takes time to discover the authentic energy of desire.

Recently, Steve called to ask if I might help him take his photography hobby "to the next level." Over the years, he has had a series of intermittent love affairs with the camera, during which time his efforts showed signs of artistic promise. But whenever Steve reached the point where commitment to his art was needed, he summarily abandoned the relationship.

At our first meeting, Steve seems totally baffled by his inability to stick with his goal. I ask him to tell me what it means to be an artist. Quickly becoming animated, Steve relays larger-than-life fantasies about becoming famous, making lots of money, and living in a big house. Not once does he mention anything about the process of taking pictures, or the kind of things he feels drawn to photograph, or even what first moved him to want to take pictures.

Here is an example of someone who is in the grip of a desire that, at heart, weakens him. Steve's longing for fame and fortune simply isn't compelling enough to enable him to stick with the rigors of becoming a working artist.

I can see from his photographs that Steve really does have a unique

[Handwritten note at top: What is your heart asking you to do?. What does your heart want? It wants to play, piddle, spend the time in openess to find the hidden treasures, the secrets of God hidden in secret places — My heart wants to create what God pours through me]

vision and a genuine talent for capturing haunting images. I ask Steve to close his eyes and visualize the part of himself that is *already* an artist: "Ask him what HE wants," I prompt.

Steve spends subsequent sessions questioning and listening to himself in a way he never has before. I ask Steve to continue these conversations in a journal so he can practice and develop a new habit of communicating with his inner artist. This simple technique helps him diminish his surface preoccupation with acclaim, focusing his attention on something deeper—his desire to communicate through photographic images.

[Handwritten note in right margin: My desire to know help others know God through journaling in color Drawing Near Praying in Color Turning Insides Out]

Steve's new intimacy with himself connects him with a deep desire to take responsibility for his heart and what it is asking him to do. When his fears surface, we use this same dialogue strategy for naming and facing them. Afterwards, Steve feels empowered and proud. He slowly develops a new vision for his life, grounded in the value of pursuing his passion for its own sake. Making money at what he loves is a worthwhile goal, but letting go of grandiose expectations for the future means Steve feels less pressure in the present. Lightening the weight of his emotional baggage empowers Steve to shift a lifelong pattern of avoidance and embrace genuine feelings of desire.

······ ·· ●

The vibrancy of creative desire is part of the same life-force energy found in everything in the natural world. The flow of desire can feel as natural as breathing. But many of us never learn how to connect to it or direct it in a satisfying way. Consequently, the force of desire can sometimes frighten and attract simultaneously, triggering a potent mix of complex feelings: excitement, motivation, optimism, happiness, confidence, aggression, greed, frustration, fear, shame, or destructive impulsivity.

For years, I wasted the energies of desire because I did not have the ability to quiet myself in order to identify and then focus my passions constructively. I lived in a constant whirl in which my desire manifested itself superficially in the drama of youthful rebellion, experimentation, and romantic distraction. I fancied myself to be fully alive, while the rest of the world languished in a dreary conventional existence. In reality, I was misdirecting valuable emotional energy, making it impossible for me to connect with who I really was and what I really wanted. What I sought was meaning and an outlet for its expression, but I couldn't tolerate the deep connection and slowness of pace that the cultivation of meaning requires.

Many creators possess a strong emotional nature. Whether we act out our emotions as I did, or act them *in*, by repressing and restricting the body's natural flow of feeling, the end result is similar. If we can't connect with our desires, decipher their meaning, and channel their energy effectively, then the force of desire ends up controlling us.

When I finally wore myself out, I started questioning the way I had been implementing the early lessons of my life. In so doing, I took my first meaningful steps in learning how to contain the flow of my passions.

······•

We cannot maintain relationships, let alone achieve our goals, without exerting self-control over the mind's incessant stream of impulse and desire. Early and sometimes painful lessons in delaying gratification are part of the normal process of socialization that begins before we can even speak. Unfortunately, in accomplishing this task, many of us don't necessarily develop actual skills to *contact, contain, and channel* emotional energy productively. Instead, out of fear, we instinctively constrict our bodies in an attempt to shut off the flow of sensation. Maybe we do find our place as responsible and productive members of society—but over time, the signal of *authentic desire* becomes so weak we scarcely know it is there. Without realizing how it happened, we wake up one day to find ourselves standing outside of our own lives, resigned, and diminished.

Containment becomes an important strategy for helping creators manage emotion, especially strong emotions like desire. When we learn to *contain*, instead of constrict, restrict, or act out, we can experience intensity of emotion, stay engaged with our process, and channel emotional vibrancy into our work.

A way of being that contains and nurtures the intensity of desire looks something like this:

We become quiet and surround our aspirations with a secure field of acceptance and love. Then we find a safe place inside ourselves where we can visit and play with our hopes and dreams, as well as examine our fears. We learn to wait and be patient with ourselves. We stop forcing solutions. We focus instead on healing the constricted places in our psyches in order to grow strong enough and clear enough to act.

······˙··●

From a spiritual perspective, desire expresses our heart's longing for union with the self and beyond. It is the deep need to direct our energies and talents toward meaningful ends. If we permit our doubts and our fears—of intimacy, abandonment, loss of control, or failure— to go unchallenged, we will turn away from the intense engagement, the demands for new learning, and the considered sacrifice that the creative process requires. It took me a long, long time to tame my restless passions, to step away from my outwardly adventurous life, to abandon surface excitement in favor of a deeper and more fulfilling— yet more demanding—relationship with myself and the world. It has been both the hardest thing I have ever done, and the best.

When you embrace your heart's desire, you must be prepared to welcome and work with everything that lies within your heart—loneliness, grief, depression, anger, fear, shame, joy, passion, tenderness, generosity, forgiveness, gratitude, courage—all of it.

Learning to acknowledge desire is the first step in the creative process. Once you allow yourself to want something badly enough, the force of your wanting will give you the strength to open the door to inner resources you simply can't see until you take that first step.

Listen. Listen to that small stubborn voice loving you in secret; it beckons you to a new world. *Are you ready?*

Speak Lord for your servant is listening

Further Reflections On Desire

The desire to create is one of the deepest yearnings of the human soul. If you wish to go deeper, explore one or more of the following questions. *Write, draw, dance, paint, meditate . . .*

☞ Am I satisfied with how I spend my days? If not, what do I want?

☞ Do I frequently feel overwhelmed by competing desires? Which of my desires are strong, which are weak, and which seem to contradict each other? Upon reflection, which desires matter most?

☞ When do I feel most alive? What do I see when I close my eyes and imagine living my truest life? What am I longing to create? If I could sing my song, what would the title be?

☞ Where do I settle for less because I'm afraid I can't have what I want? Do I focus too much on fulfilling the desires of others while neglecting my own?

☛ Upon reflection, which of my desires are inspired by externals like advertising—or by what others expect, have, or want?

☛ Which of my desires are actually attempts to de-stress, serving as "rewards" for over-working or doing what I don't want to do? Does satisfying these desires help or hinder my creativity?

☛ What helps me gather up the courage to walk away from things I *want,* but don't *need,* in order to focus on what truly matters?

☛ What deep yearnings still hover at the periphery of my life? What desires have I given up because I'm afraid to fail?

☛ In what ways do I squander valuable emotional energy that could be directed into fulfilling my dreams?

☛ How can I cultivate my heart's desire? What habits and practices nourish my dreams?

☛ What brings meaning to my life? What gives me pleasure on a daily basis? Where do meaning and pleasure overlap for me? If they don't, what prevents me from finding pleasure *in* meaning and well-being?

*Dare to vision . . . whatever is birthed out of the dark
can only do so if we have been able to imagine it.*

—Joanna Macy

*So you see, imagination needs moodling–long,
inefficient, happy idling, dawdling and puttering.*

—Brenda Ueland

*Logic will take you from A to B but imagination will
take you everywhere else.*

—Albert Einstein

Imagination

ONE OF MY FAVORITE PASTIMES as a child is gazing up at cloud-filled
skies. I float through a billowy wonderland among fanciful animal
companions. Imagination is my best friend, offering me a world where
I can find relief from my great loneliness.

Now that I am all grown up, my idea of heaven is a large picture
window with an expansive view. Given my druthers, I enjoy whiling
away my days in idle reverie. I admit to feeling some guilt about my
love of repose since the cultural consensus disparages "doing nothing"
as a waste of time. But navigating the creative process requires an
interesting blend of active and passive qualities. If we are too dreamy,
then we can't get off the couch to do the work of creation—but the
opposite is also true. When we are in constant motion, our active
lives fill us to overflowing and there is no room for anything new to

see back of book

be born. Creativity blossoms from fantasy, daydreams, and from time that is slow, careless, and, above all, unstructured. *Creativity thrives in the space between our efforts.*

......·..•

Imagination supports our dreams. The other night I drifted in a soft, drowsy space just before sleep and I caught a glimpse of my finished book. This is what I saw: *A large title with sensual letters making a graceful sweep across the cover, surrounded by colorful shapes. Red, yellow, orange, pink, green dance around a swirl of black. Contained within each colorful form are small white letters that proclaim some of the oh-so-wild ideas inside. And then, the quickening of my pulse in delicious anticipation. Yes! There* WILL *be a book.*

The cover I have just described may not be the cover of the book you hold in your hand. The point is not to get it *right*; imagination is not a perfect prognosticator. *The purpose of imagination is to play with possibilities.* The beauty of the mind's eye lies in its experimental freedom. The fluidity of imagination allows impulse to become form, dissolve into feeling, and become form again, for as long as it takes until it is time to act. Remember, at this point in the process you don't need to have anything resolved. No decisions or commitments are required. Imagination is not about doing. *It's about the willingness to see.*

......·..•

One sure way to scare yourself stuck and suffocate your imagination is by thinking two little words—*be realistic.* The monster of common sense feeds on the succulent juices of newly hatched ideas.

My client Jennifer wants to use her skills as a personal trainer in a more creative context by building a training facility on a portion of her

DREAM

WHAT IF ???

12-9-19
"Bobbi Houston's book is not a coincidence - it is dots colliding with your here + now - her heart with your desire to teach them HOW TO DRAW NEAR - Don't shrink back Sunshine - Don't shrink back - Press on towards the prize Press on - there is a WORLD full of hurting, lonely, broken, lost people that need to be taught that I AM REAL + that there is a WAY to find Me"

Whimsy Joy Faith

country property. While Jennifer's eyes remain closed and inwardly focused on the pictures created by her imagination, she describes a quiet and beautifully designed space, an intimate garden oasis where harried individuals could come during the day to relax, tone, and rejuvenate their spirits as well as their bodies. It's a splendid and nourishing alternative to the crowded, musclebound weight-lifting clubs in town. I sense this is truly a heartfelt desire, because Jennifer's face radiates enthusiasm as she speaks. But in the brief space of time it takes for her to open her eyes, Jennifer's practical mind asserts itself, rattling off a litany of commentary that appears to doom the proposal from the start. "What a stupid idea! No one will drive that far. Didn't someone already try that and fail? What about permits? It sounds too expensive, not to mention impractical. . . ."

Jennifer's *practical mind* has no interest in listening to her *creative mind*. And her creative mind can't field the barrage of questions being leveled against it. In a matter of moments, Jennifer's shoulders slump forward, followed by her head, which hangs down as if from a shameful rebuke. The monster of common sense strikes again, devouring Jennifer's idea before it can hatch.

We all can relate to Jennifer's dilemma.

Most of us have a highly developed sense of what is reasonable and what is not. Memory of our previous experiences can determine the boundaries of what we believe possible. The unfamiliar ends up being relentlessly scrutinized for potential complications as the mind generates unlimited disaster scenarios. Sometimes these conclusions are accurate and sometimes they are not. Indeed, many of them are based on the erroneous assumption that what is true in the past will be true for the future. Much lies outside our range of expertise. Imagination dreams beyond our limited perceptions and experience to help us consider something we may never have thought of before—to show us what might lie beyond the boundaries of our known world.

······∙∙●

Here's one way of working with your creative imagination. First, *picture* your mind as a playing field—a safe place away from the eyes of the world where you can begin the process of turning the vagaries of feeling into something tangible. Now, surround your field with things you like. Plant some flowers around it. How about a couple of trees for climbing? You remember those old friendly oaks, the ones with branches like big fat arms, holding you high and safe? And don't forget to paint the sky overhead in your favorite colors. Purple is definitely okay. Next, stand in the middle of your field. *Notice* how solid the ground is beneath your feet. You are being held. *Sense* the spirit here. *Breathe* in the fresh, clean air. *Open* out your arms. Wider. *Smell* the breeze as it caresses your skin. *Feel* yourself extending out into all the possibilities awaiting you. *Dare* to imagine them.

Are you able to enter this vision in your mind? Are you surprised? Pleased? How long does it take before a negative thought, like "This is so stupid," interrupts your process?

······∙∙●

Because the practical mind communicates its agenda with such certainty and quickness of force, the fragile threads that weave an untested vision will frequently give way under the glare of intense and relentless scrutiny. During the early stages of the creative process, you may never be able to fully justify what you dream because the pictures the imagination creates consist of gossamer and glitter. Don't assume that their fragility or strangeness indicates anything about their viability. Even a nebulous idea can be nurtured into substantial outcomes, if you believe in yourself. When imagination joins desire and determination, you will be amazed by what you can accomplish.

•••••·•••●

Another way you can encourage your power of imagination is by
listening. Your heart is always whispering stories. Hearing them awakens
your mind's natural ability to make pictures. Do you remember the
pleasure of "story time" when you were a child? When the active work
of learning—having to figure things out, having to answer questions—
gave way to the delights of receiving? Story time was an opportunity to
sit back and do nothing but listen.

Remember what it was like to listen? Picture yourself putting your
head down on your desk or lying on your mat. The teacher puts her
finger to her lips. "Hush, now," she says. As she begins reading, a gradual
wave of quiet descends over the room. You feel yourself softening but
also becoming more alert. You are listening intently because you want
to know what will happen next. In your mind's eye, you quickly find
yourself stepping into the story. Watch it unfold in the privacy of your
imagination. Sense the excitement of uncertainty in your body. Will the
prince rescue the princess in time?

Remember the freedom of accepting wholeheartedly, of simply
waiting for the story to evolve, of becoming so engaged that you forgot
all about what happened on the playground during recess? Remember
listening for the simple pleasure of listening, without an agenda, without waiting for the opportunity to speak? Ask yourself: *What do I need
to listen to right now?*

•••••·•••●

Every new idea generates problems that cry out for resolution.
That's the nature of creativity. But the demand for premature solutions
will shut off the creative flow. That's not to say there isn't a point in the
process where you must be mindful of reality. Part of what makes it

possible to complete what you start is the ability to identify problems, generate and evaluate alternatives, and then make a decision. It's just that now isn't the time.

So relax, there will be plenty of room for applying that practical intellect you're so fond of later on. For now, open your mind and heart. Nurture your hopes and aspirations. Slow down, so you can give yourself the time and space to dream. Listen to the energy in your body. Experience the rush of possibility. Let your imagination be a window onto your desires. And then . . . sit back and take in the view.

Further Reflections On Imagination

Knowledge is limited to what you currently know. *Imagination* can take you beyond the limits of the known world. If you wish to go deeper, explore one or more of the following questions. *Write, draw, dance, paint, meditate . . .*

☞ What inspires my imagination? (The unexpected? The beauty of everyday? Nature? A multi-sensory environment packed with ideas? The relics of the past? Trying something new? My relationships and sense of community?)

☞ What areas of my life suffer from a lack of inspired vision? How does that affect me?

☞ How do I use the power of my imagination? (As a constructive tool for problem solving? To visualize possibility? To escape into fantasy? Or do I spend way too much time using my imagination to scare myself with what-if disaster scenarios?) to bless for joy *not worth the effort, doing it / too many already / upset life & family*

➤ What criticisms do I direct at myself to stifle my imagination? How does negative thinking protect me from the failure I fear is coming?

➤ How do I feel when I imagine the best outcome for my vision?

unstoppable   excited

➤ If I imagine myself living a creatively expressive life, what do I see? (Which desires emerge to be lived? What dreams seek fulfillment?)

➤ Consider Rumi: "Out beyond ideas of wrongdoing and rightdoing there is a field. I'll meet you there."

What in your life is calling you? When all the noise is silenced, the meetings adjourned, the lists laid aside, and the wild iris blooms by itself in the dark forest, what still pulls on your soul?

—Nancy Goddard and Colleen Kelly

There's something great and useful I could be doing, and that I don't know what it is hangs over me like some major errand I know I'm meant to do.

—Anne Lamott

Purpose is all that separates adversity from adventure, boredom from profound motivation.

—Jeff Saltz

Purpose

TO LOVE WHAT YOU DO and feel that it matters—what could be more satisfying? When you live in tune with the purpose of your life, you can harness the wild, vibrant energy of creative desire and direct it to meaningful ends.

Your purpose reflects the essence of who you are. Purpose channels creative energy in a thousand ways, large and small, and finds expression in as many directions as there are possibilities. Purpose can help a homeless stranger find a job, or build a flagging credit union into a solvent institution that enables thousands of working people to obtain low-interest loans. Purpose can make colorful handcrafted teapots that give pleasure to the eye, plant a community vegetable garden, design a structure that elegantly meets the needs of its occupants, or bake a pie to enter in the county fair. Purpose finds expression whenever you focus your creative energy to do the things you know you were born to do.

I don't know about you, but I've always admired (and secretly envied) people who know from an early age why they are here and where they are headed. Possessing a palpable sense of their future, these iconic individuals construct plans and actually follow them to positive results. As a young woman, still mostly a child, on the verge of finding my own way, I longed for the relief of certainty, for the reassurance that comes from knowing who I am, knowing that I matter, knowing what matters—and, how to manifest it. But that sort of natural self-assurance and social ease is not my style. Trial and error—or should I say trial and *terror*—is my bailiwick.

·······•

Each of us must travel our own path to discover who we truly are and how we can best express that uniqueness in the world. My girlish senses marinate for a decade or more in fantastical, glossy media images of suburban *Leave It to Beaver* domesticity that reflect a woman's purpose in the 1950s and 60s. Smiling, perfectly coiffed, pearl-draped, high-heel-clad mothers clean their floors and serve meals to their families—all apparently fulfilled in their effortless domesticity.

I find it very confusing.

In real life, my mother is obese, unkempt, and undone by the unrelenting demands of homemaking. The power of her unfocused passions overwhelms her capacity to take care of herself, let alone the rest of us. She's up, she's down, she runs round and round, getting little accomplished. My only control lies inside my own mind. My only prayer consists of a VOW → MY LIFE will accomplish a substantial purpose.

·······•

My father shows me how to stand up in this world. Passionate about his calling as a physician, he directs his prodigious energies to the healing arts. Rarely does he arrive home before eight o'clock at night. Too often the phone rings as soon as he steps into the house. After pouring himself yet another of the many cups of coffee he consumes throughout his long day, he stoically walks out the door to make a house call. My father prides himself on his dedication. He delivers a level of personalized service seldom seen in modern medicine's increasingly bureaucratic maze of paperwork and cost cutting. Frankly, I resent the fact that I never see enough of him. Nevertheless, I am proud to be his daughter. He does important work in this world; he saves lives. My father's life inspires me to my own purpose: I also want to make a positive difference in the lives of others.

But . . .

How can I possibly follow my father? Everyone says he is a genius. I am not a genius. Certainly, I am not as book-smart as he is. He can sit for hours studying and reading and memorizing bits and pieces of information. He recites Shakespeare from memory; I can barely remember my phone number. I do well enough in school, but it's a struggle. I like to read, but I don't like to sit and study. He spends long periods of his life following a rigorous and highly disciplined path, a well-worn trail blazed by others who preceded him. I try to live up to his example, but his path does not suit my adventurous temperament and sensibilities. He means well, but he doesn't really understand me or accept our differences. I don't see myself in him and I don't want to see myself in my mother, so I can't see myself at all.

I feel perplexed. I've figured out that my purpose is "to make a difference," but how will I fulfill it? I must have some abilities. I don't know what they are, but I sense that they are there. I don't know how I will discover them. I don't know where they are going to lead me but wherever that is, I have to follow, even if it is down a series of blind alleys until I find one that opens onto the rest of my life. I require freedom—freedom my father never allowed himself—to take this particular journey in my own fashion. We clash like dueling titans, locked in an epic battle that he only reluctantly concedes once I succeed in finding my own way—beyond the limits of his imagination.

······ ·· ●

Like many men of his generation, my goal-oriented father didn't distinguish between *purpose* and *goal*. Purpose tends to remain at bedrock, even as goals shift, reflecting the diverse context of our lives. While goals can change throughout life, purpose remains the fundamental organizing principle around which everything in life resolves, whether we are conscious of it or not. Indeed, purpose determines the very nature of our goals. Picture a wheel. At the center lies purpose. The spokes radiating outward represent individual goals, each finding its own direction, all originating from the same core purpose.

······ ·· ●

Each of us has a life purpose to which we can apply our creative energy, and we have already undergone many of the experiences we need to prepare us for that purpose. Everything becomes a resource. As creators, we use whatever has happened to us as raw material to shape our creative lives—including our humiliations, our misfortunes, our embarrassments. All forms of madness, bizarre habits, personality quirks, and awkwardness find expression—and hence purpose—when we create from them. Sometimes we must dig out from under a landslide of outmoded beliefs, early conditioning, emotional wounding, and inappropriate fantasies; sometimes we must struggle to bring the disparate snapshots of experience into a coherent whole of understanding.

There are many paths that will assist you in this quest. All these paths have the potential to help you clarify who you are, what you believe in, and what you have to contribute to the world. Some people, like my father, choose the scholarly approach through institutions of higher learning; others prefer the bohemian route and follow the call of the open road in search of real-life experience; still others take a spiritual path of meditation, quiet retreat, and community service. For many, the answer lies in pursuing personal growth options like counseling, workshops, and self-help workbooks. I have found that a combination of any and all of these can be useful. Whatever path calls to you, follow it with heartfelt intention and it will lead you home to yourself and your purpose.

······· ●

Purpose answers the soul's longing for meaning. In an increasingly uncertain world, the soul-reach of purpose becomes a sustaining source of nourishment, comfort, and focus during those long lonely stretches of creative work when doubt threatens to overwhelm our progress (and at times our sanity). Like a compass pointing the way north, purpose remains the one constant that helps maintain a sense of continuity when we feel confused, frightened, or when confronting difficult choices.

It is never too late to realize who you really are and why you are here. Even if you have spent years misdirecting your energies, you are never too old to begin the journey. And when we finally cease from all our worldly dramas and diversions, we can return home to discover something precious that has been patiently awaiting our arrival.

Further Reflections On Purpose

In her poem, "The Summer Day," Mary Oliver famously asks, "What is it you plan to do with your one wild and precious life?" If you wish to go deeper, explore one or more of the following questions. Your responses to these inquiries provide insight into the person you are at the core of your being and clues as to how you might direct your creative energy. *Write, draw, dance, paint, meditate . . .*

- What values and experiences have helped shape me into the person I am becoming or have become? *Conversion Friendships: Cindy WCBS Family, internet Teacher Books*

- For what hidden purpose could my deepest losses and disappointments be preparing me? *Help others draw near to God*

- What did I love as a child? How might I infuse those passions into my life today? *Scrapbooking dreaming exercise*

- What do I really want—artistically, personally, professionally?

- What gives my body energy? What ideas, situations, and circumstances draw me inexplicably? *walking laughter God's presence discipline music color - Friendships creativity*

- What moments in my life stand out as peak experiences? What do I wish to communicate to others as a result of these experiences?

- What brings me deep joy? What do I care most about? To what extent do I spend my time doing what I value?

☞ What ideas, feelings, or images seem to revisit me again and again
   even though I keep turning away from them?

☞ If I could get paid for doing anything I wanted, what would I choose?

Research   Piddling on computer   Piddling in MSR

☞ What are my gifts? In what ways might these gifts serve the world?

☞ What is my secret dream?

*We need to view ourselves with the same curiosity
and openness with which we study a tree, the sky or a
thought because we are linked to the entire universe.*

—Henri Matisse

*I'm a vagabond, curious about everything,
entering everywhere.*

—Federico Fellini

*Don't refuse to go on an occasional
wild goose chase.*

—Henry S. Haskins

Curiosity

I DREAM OFTEN of my farm in Sonoma County. Those halcyon,
light-filled days come upon me in the dark REM of sleep . . .

*I am young again. I live with a large menagerie of animals, including
my llama, Geraldo. We're up and out on the road a bit earlier than usual
this morning for our walk with Gus, canine companion and resident rabble
rouser. While Gus bounds along recklessly, barreling into tall grasses, sniffing
haphazardly in search of hidden messages, Geraldo saunters regally with
a serene bearing. With large blue-brown eyes, he gazes intently, absolutely
transfixed by whatever he sees. Inquisitive, alert, and present to the moment,
he is the embodiment of curiosity.*

Like animals, children show a keen interest in their surroundings
purely for the joy of discovery. When we are young, curiosity is a
natural response to feeling related and connected to everything in the

universe. The sky is not something blue and high and far away; we become that sky . . . we too are wide and clear and vast.

Recall those spacious childhood perceptions that permitted you to ask luminous questions: *If a bird eats a cocoon, will it turn into a butterfly? Where does the sky sleep at night? What is the color of the wind? What was before the beginning?*

In adulthood, your creative journey can begin with the same impulse to wonder: *What would happen if I worked at something I loved? What does it mean to lead a simple life? Why do I keep doing that to him, to her, to myself? What if I started to play the piano? How can I capture the quality of light streaming through the window? How do I give form to nuance and impulse? Could it work if I were willing to let go of that?*

·····'··●

Curiosity—asking questions—is the means by which we consider the richness of possibility. But, frequently, the kinds of *intimidating* questions we ask ourselves do more to close the door on potential than to open it. The key is to dare to ask *provocative* questions—these are the kind of questions that empower our thinking beyond the narrow confines of fear.

Robert comes to see me with an all too common dilemma: His life is consumed by a financially lucrative but creatively dead-end job. "I am desperate to make a change," he confesses.

I ask him if he has a sense of what else he wants to do. Immediately, he launches into a passionate discourse describing how he has always wanted to combine his love of travel with public policy issues—a far cry from his current position as vice-president of a brokerage firm.

While his *heart* waxes effusively about its true desires, Robert's *mind* keeps interrupting to ask scary questions that tend to limit the scope of inquiry: *Will I be able to keep my house? Will my children have to attend public school? Will my wife have to go back to work?* Despite the intensity of his longing, Robert has difficulty being curious about what his heart is trying to tell him; his frightened mind causes him to focus immediately and exclusively on all the possible costs of the decision.

Robert's reaction is something I see over and over again in people who claim to be uncreative. As soon as a new possibility arises, it is immediately attacked by a barrage of negative questions and counter-arguments. Remember Jennifer from the earlier section about Imagination? Like Jennifer, Robert responds to his own ideas as if they are marauding invaders from whom he must protect himself. Although he begins the session sincerely seeking an alternative to his less-than-satisfying life-style, Robert takes up arms against that alternative as soon as it appears.

······⸱··●

Curiosity can lead us to new knowledge and a broader sense of our-selves. Unfortunately, for many of us, the mere suggestion of something new seems to threaten the sense of control we have over our lives. Like Robert, we erect defenses so quickly that we don't give ourselves space to fall in love with our ideas, much less time to work them out. If we want to open our lives and make room for our deepest desires, culti-vating the quality of curiosity can help us find a compromise between our attachment to security and predictability and the longings of our passionate nature.

I invite Robert to approach himself the way a llama would. "Try to move toward your heart with gentle interest," I offer. "Instead of cutting yourself off, why not consider the kind of open and evocative questions that will enable you to hear your own inner guidance?"

What are my values and how well does my current lifestyle reflect them? Can my quality of life improve if I take a job that pays less money but is more in tune with those values? How can my children benefit from my example and what lessons are they learning from my current choices? What are the strengths of my marriage and how can they sustain my relationship through this change? Why am I so afraid? How might this change bring me a greater security beyond what I know today?

Human nature compels us to protect ourselves by becoming less inquisitive when we feel threatened. When we make the decision to live our lives creatively, however, we discover again and again that apparently frightening consequences can lead to a richer life. And the very places and questions we turn away from offer exactly what we need to proceed to the next level of development.

·······˙··●

Robert feels scared but determined. Our sessions continue as he confronts his anxiety about changing his life. Together, we process many of his deep-seated survival fears, including experiences of early abandonment by his father, who left the family to pursue his own passions. Although they are deeply painful, Robert confronts the feelings associated with this early loss. He learns to separate past events from his current adult life, empowering him to make the necessary tradeoffs for the sake of a more meaningful life, without repeating the earlier trauma.

The remedy for a stagnant life is a curious mind that investigates whatever compels, interests, hurts, or threatens. In this way, we eventually find exactly what we need in order to fulfill ourselves. It is an unsettling truth that what attracts us often scares us, but it is also true that what scares us may also love us. Curiosity enables creators to complete the circle from desire to fear to love. And once we fall in love, we are more likely to do whatever it takes to bring our vision to life.

·······˙··●

Ultimately, a curious mind frees us from our rigid and dogmatic ways of perceiving reality. A man once told Picasso that he ought to make pictures of things "the way they are." When Picasso said he did not understand, the man showed him a photograph of his wife and said, "There, you see, this is a picture of how she really is."

Picasso replied, "She is rather small, isn't she? And flat?"

Of course, Picasso could reproduce objective reality quite well, but it was his great curiosity that led him to explore the deeper dimensions of things and discover a new way of seeing and painting.

Curiosity refuses to be bound by the narrow consideration of the way things are. Instead, a curious mind explores the endlessly evolving ways that we can see and feel the world around us. For the creator, curiosity energizes the whole of life by moving us closer to mystery and to that which we will never fully comprehend. In a creative life, there is no lasting conclusion, no end to questioning, and no stopping place for the curious mind—just plateaus with breathtaking views. For whatever answers we do find become the seeds of tomorrow's questions.

Further Reflections On Curiosity

Curiosity is the engine of the creative process—it's what drives you to keep learning and growing beyond your limits. If you wish to go deeper, explore one or more of the following questions. *Write, draw, dance, paint, meditate . . .*

☞ What grabs my curiosity?

☞ Do I possess a curious and questioning nature or do I tend to be more cautious and circumspect? Am I willing to ask dumb questions?

☞ When I talk to myself, what tone of voice do I use? How do I shoot down my ideas before giving them a real chance?

☞ In what ways does curiosity's open-ended nature disturb me? How does my lack of curiosity keep returning me to the same old perceptions, habits, and outcomes?

☞ What kinds of knowledge or experiences would I be curious about if I were immune from consequences?

☞ What are my ideas for a project I've been thinking about? What questions do I wish someone would ask me?

☞ Consider John O'Donohue: "May my mind come alive today to the invisible geography that invites me to new frontiers . . ."

*To dare is to lose one's footing momentarily. Not to
dare is to lose oneself.*

—Sören Kierkegaard

*Any person who makes the commitment to the
pursuit of something meaningful is at risk.*

—Bob Shacochis

*Our lives improve only when we take chances
and the first most difficult risk we can take
is to be honest with ourselves.*

—Walter Anderson

Risk

I AM SEATED AT A TABLE in a ballroom so huge I can barely see the
other end of the room. My heart pounds—BOOMDADABOOM-
DADABOOM—and my chest seems about to explode all over the
beautiful parquet floor. What I thought were butterflies in my stomach
have mutated into locusts in a feeding frenzy.

The crowd of about three hundred managers finish their chicken
lunches. Waiters serve cheesecake and coffee as the din of conversation
fills the room around me. A man steps behind the microphone and I
see his lips moving. (I am, of course, watching all this from a parallel
universe far, far away.) And then I hear my name being called. Barely
able to stand, I start moving toward the sound of the voice. Somehow,
my legs carry me up to the podium. The room becomes deathly still.
I look out onto a sea of eyes, every one of them staring with rapt

anticipation—right at me. They say it helps to imagine the audience without clothes, but I'm the one who feels like a naked emperor. For a moment, I glance overhead and imagine the glittering crystal chandelier falling on me as a merciful reprieve from this, the most terrifying of all possible risks—public speaking.

Afterwards, instead of making the long drive home, I make plans to stay with a friend in the city. She anticipates an actual visit with a live person; but all I can do is lie there like a rag doll, staring at whatever images flicker across her TV screen. I hate the way I feel—exhausted, depleted from the day's performance. But most of all, I hate the way this work, that at first so thrilled me, that seemed so glamorous, so full of promise, and that made me feel so important, is now draining the life out of me.

The next morning I stumble out of bed and take a long look at myself in the bathroom mirror. The haggard face staring back at me silently admonishes, "You are not cut out for this line of work." There, in the greenish cast of florescent lighting, is the ghastly truth: *I'm really not.*

I had taken a chance on trying something new by branching out into consulting. Now, I had to be straight with myself: It wasn't working. I had to quit. Sometimes, the greatest risk we can take is to be honest with ourselves. It isn't easy for me to acknowledge my misgivings. And, it is even harder to face the loss of lucrative business. At first, I think bitter thoughts to myself: "You can't just quit. You're going to end up like your mother."

••••••·••●

We are so afraid of trying something and failing. We tend to condemn ourselves when we spend valuable time pursuing new avenues, only to discover that they aren't what we expected. But, chances taken that turn out badly can provide valuable perspective. Risking and failing (or just finding out that something we tried isn't right for us) can frequently open the doors to something better suited to our talents and temperament. The risks I took while working in the public eye helped to focus me on what I really wanted to be doing with my life.

After my foray into the hustle and bustle of the business world, the benefits of working at home again feel like a gift. Not only is the pace of my life more relaxed, but the intimate, one-on-one relationships I maintain with my private clients give me the opportunity to make a meaningful, long-term difference—which, after all, is really the whole purpose of my life. I feel nourished by my work in a way that I haven't for a long time.

In becoming such a public figure, I was pushing past my sensitive and introverted nature—facing down my fear and growing in the process, to be sure—but the results were not particularly satisfying in the long run. My intuitive gifts were going to waste in the corporate setting, which favors a linear, short-term approach to problem solving.

Upon reflection, it seemed to me that the risks I took on behalf of corporate consulting were, in many ways, senseless. Even though I received positive feedback for my efforts, I really wasn't making much of an impact by my own reckoning. Even worse, I simply didn't care enough about what I was doing.

In the months that follow, I move beyond my apparent failure. I realize I can fulfill my need for more connection with the outside world by taking a different kind of risk—one that offers the level of depth and reflection that I crave, one that will also prove to be enormously challenging.

I had occasionally written articles as part of my work, but now I make the decision to begin a regular writing practice. I create a small, quarterly publication and invite contributions from other artists and writers. In sending my intimate thoughts and feelings out into the world for people to read (and judge), I substitute one venue of risk for another.

·······‥•

Creators live lives of risk. A creative life is risky because the process stretches us beyond what we feel capable of doing and we don't know what will happen. The challenge lies in permitting ourselves to care deeply enough about something to make taking those risks truly worthwhile. Sometimes the greatest risk lies in acknowledging the truth of our desires.

After I have been writing for a number of years, people start asking me if I plan to write a book. I really don't believe I can write a book, but rather than admit that out loud, I tell people that I don't want to. Deep down I am afraid. I am terrified of the sheer volume of work involved, terrified of the demands such a huge responsibility will make on me; terrified of the sacrifices I will need to make. I have never given myself to any single project that big.

RAT-A-TAT-TAT>>>My fears hurl rapid-fire questions I have no way of answering.>>>*RAT-A-TAT-TAT*>>>"What if I start but can't finish?">>>*RAT-A-TAT-TAT*>>>"What if I finish and it is just plain bad?">>>*RAT-A-TAT-TAT*>>>"What if it is good but not good enough?" >>>*RAT-A-TAT-TAT*>>>"What if no one wants it?" (meaning, of course, What if no one wants ME?) *RAT-A-TAT-TAT*>>>Ack!>>No way!

Just entertaining the notion of writing a book triggers my deepest insecurities: *Am I valued? Am I good enough? Does anyone care?*

It will take a decade before my defenses will let me get within striking distance of consciously considering such a monumental risk. Another decade passes before my heart finally overrules the last of my puerile objections. But once my heart gets the better of me, there is no turning back. Like a mother about to give birth, no matter what happens, I can't walk away.

Although most of us refuse to take a risk until we are compelled by outside circumstances, it feels a whole lot better to be inspired by love. When there is enough love, we are able to act in the face of our strongest fears. And when we dare to use our strength in the service of what we love, it becomes less and less important whether or not we are afraid.

Further Reflections On Risk

Writer Ray Bradbury said, "You've got to jump off cliffs all the time and build your wings on the way down." Take a leap and explore one or more of the following questions. *Write, draw, dance, paint, meditate . . .*

- In what areas of my life does fear of making a mistake prevent me from making an attempt?

- Would I rather take a risk and regret it, or do nothing and regret it? Am I running away or moving towards something?

- What kinds of risks have I taken in the past? What worked? What were the benefits of having tried even if it didn't turn out as expected?

- What would I risk if I knew I couldn't fail? What sacrifices might I need to make? What is the best outcome for taking this risk?

- What is the smallest step I can make in the direction of what I love? What is my support system for taking this risk?

And the day came

when the risk to remain tight in the bud

was more painful than the risk it took to blossom.

—*Anaïs Nin*

*In creating, the only hard thing is to begin; a grass
blade is no easier to make than an oak.*

—James Russell Lowell

*Nothing will ever be attempted if all possible
objections must first be overcome.*

—Samuel Johnson

Leap and a net will appear.

—Julia Cameron

2
Getting
Started

*O*NCE WE HAVE HEARD THE CALL from within, we cannot
continue life as it was before. Sometimes we carry our
secret longings for years. But it is not enough just to know
what we want; eventually we need to respond to that knowing. Sooner
or later we must begin.

Getting started can be difficult. It's one thing to have an idea; most
people have lots of them. It's quite another matter to rouse those sleepy
aspirations from the safe haven of our own private dreamworld in order to
put them to work creating something real. We tend to abandon our most
cherished yearnings to the dusty back rooms of the unconscious because
we are so daunted by the leap from conception to actualization.

The problem with starting is that we often want to be finished before
we even begin. We become so anxious about the uncertainties inherent in
beginnings that we avoid putting our attention where it needs to be—on
the question we are trying to answer, on the problem we are endeavoring to

solve. Instead, our creative energy becomes dissipated as we obsess about our inadequacies, worry about possible rejection and failure, or become lost in euphoric dreams of glory. At other times, our fears cause us to grasp desperately at uninspired approaches.

Moving from the abstractions of the mind's eye into a full-bodied engagement with the physical realm often triggers a howling of internal protest. The frightening gap between the two worlds of mind and matter cries out to be filled. As we gaze upon this abyss, we begin to feel nervous. There is, after all, the constant threat of falling in, not to mention a naked loneliness.

No matter, we need to begin anyway. We need to take hold of ourselves—along with our aspirations and trepidations—and cross the threshold laughing, crying, kicking, and screaming. Ask yourself: *Is there something I am willing to start today despite my reluctance?*

The principal work of beginning is to lay the groundwork. We are not trying to grow, make, or solve anything at this point, as much as we are preparing and opening ourselves for the period of creative productivity still to come. Our task is to hold the question in our minds; turning it over and around and sideways, considering it from every conceivable angle. To this end, we must learn to manage interruptions and quiet the cacophony of voices in order to cultivate the kind of wholehearted absorption and intentionality that attracts potential resources to the problem.

Qualities that prepare the ground for successful beginnings include *concentration, discovery, learning, chaos, and commitment.*

Concentration contacts, holds, and focuses the problem internally. *Discovery* opens us to the world, making connections and gathering input on possible solutions. *Learning* challenges and changes us while laying the foundation for growth, mastery, and future accomplishment. *Chaos* embraces multiple options at once, fertilizing the creative ground. *Commitment* fortifies our capacity to finish what we start.

Concentration is the secret of strength.

—Ralph Waldo Emerson

*I owe everything to the close union of solitude and
silence, to a passionate and exclusive attention
akin to hypnosis.*

—Claude Monet

Sit at your desk and listen . . .

—Franz Kafka

Concentration

OKAY, SO YOU'RE STRUCK by a brilliant idea. . . . *You're up! You're excited!
You're ready to push up your sleeves and give it your undivided attention.
You grab a cup of coffee and sit down at your desk. You turn on the computer
or pick up a pen, pencils, and pad intending to make some notes or preliminary
sketches. Glancing up momentarily, you find yourself staring out the window
into the garden. It's a beautiful day. The sun and chaise longue beckon but
you resist the temptation. A fleeting thought drifts in, reminding you that it's
time to deadhead the roses, so you write yourself a note. You try again to
concentrate on the idea. After a few minutes, you suddenly remember a
friend's message you never returned from two weeks ago. Your mind becomes
riddled with guilt so you decide to call her. Forty minutes later you get off the
phone and your dog appears, leash in mouth. You'd better take him out for*

*his morning constitutional. Thirty minutes later you come home and try it
again. But you can't think straight because your stomach begins growling.
Better eat something. An hour later (you might as well catch up on emails
while you eat, right?) you go back to work, but now you are beginning to feel
slightly panicked. Your thoughts jump wildly from one thing to the next; you
begin to think that you will never be able to do it. Clouds of despair and
hopelessness begin to gather. The day that had started with such bright
promise turns quietly dark.*

Quick! What distraction will you reach for next?

So much for good intentions.

If this scene feels embarrassingly familiar, take comfort in the fact
that you are not alone. The moment we try to begin, something in us
rebels against the *effort* of concentration. It goes by many names—
*inner child, free spirit, restless mind, feral mind, monkey mind, mind chatter,
laziness.* Whatever you want to call it, it's an aspect of human nature
that resists being controlled, preferring to roam at whim rather than
harness its energies to a specific aim.

We frequently see *the rebel* as a romantic figure—the lone antihero
who fights injustice, bucks established thinking, and takes action while
others remain complacent. Many creators possess these vital qualities.
But without a counterbalance, the rebel's indiscriminate drive to agitate
will distract you and disrupt the work you long to accomplish, leaving
you feeling frustrated and demoralized.

It seems much easier, and certainly more fun, to indulge this wayward
aspect of yourself. But if you want to get started on a project, if you
desire to make any progress, you must bring purposeful and penetrating
consideration to your project. Much about creation lies outside of your
control—you cannot will inspiration, intuition, synchronistic connection, or the dawning of sudden insight. But unless you first learn to
concentrate, those things will not come.

......·..●

Many of us fail, even before we begin, because we simply cannot bring ourselves to think deeply enough. In the process of holding, turning, and mulling over the problem, information combines and recombines until something clicks. For *conceptual* creators, an idea will hatch complete in the creator's mind. *Process* creators, on the other hand, tend to harvest random elements. There might be an overall vision, but the details for bringing their ideas to fruition will be worked out in real time—as they proceed through the subsequent stages of the creative process. *Which style of creative concentration resonates with you?*

......·..●

A widespread myth claims that the true artist creates effortlessly and spontaneously. In fact, the complex process of creativity alternately requires periods of abandon and attention. While we need to be open and expressive with our feelings, while we need to be alert and responsive in the moment, the workhorse of the creative process is a discerning and disciplined mind.

I am thinking about a client of mine who can create as long as it doesn't require sustained reflection. Arlene knits colorful sweaters while watching television. But when she felt the urge to write stories based on her family's lively ethnic history, Arlene came up against the limits of her distracted style.

At age sixty, Arlene is an energetic, practical woman not given to introspection. She comes from a large family that built a successful family business through hard work and clan loyalty. That left little time to cultivate subjective experience. From an early age, Arlene ignored her own ideas and perceptions in order to be embraced by the comforting security of family norms and expectations. After decades of leading an unexamined life, she is terrified by the prospect of looking inside her own mind and heart. The ability to think creatively has everything to do with feeling free to follow the trail of personal thoughts wherever they may lead. If Arlene truly desires to take her creativity to the next level, she needs to become more comfortable with her inner life.

The art of writing requires that Arlene learn to sit quietly and penetrate what she calls "the noise in my head" in order to hear the many voices that have something important to say about Arlene's experience of family. Our work together consists of introducing her to individual members of that chaotic chorus, in addition to giving Arlene tools for contemplating and sorting through their various agendas. Arlene learns to work constructively with her inner team. She tames her outward impulsivity, tracks her thoughts, and breaks new ground in trusting herself—even when that means questioning cherished family norms. As Arlene relies less on external sources of validation and approval, she begins to write her stories. The other day I asked her how she was doing. She answered with a broad grin, "I feel truly alive for the first time in my life."

······∙∙●

When we concentrate deeply, we can wander along the mind's passageways for hours, meeting no one but ourselves. Depending on our relationship to solitude, this state may feel either nourishing or perilous. Solitude can give birth to the original in us, "to beauty unfamiliar" as author Thomas Mann wrote.

But our emotional life frequently intrudes into the spaciousness of silence: Unfinished business from the past or current worries, preoccupations, and uncertainties may interfere with the ability to concentrate. We seek distraction from these unanswered concerns by turning to activity, personal drama, or our phones for reassurance.

In our distracted age, we have lost the capacity to tolerate solitude. Unfortunately, too many of us can relate to writer Anne Lamott's quip, "My mind remains a bad neighborhood that I try not to go into alone." Sometimes we need to do some healing before we can feel safe and free enough in ourselves to create. When we transform our relationship with solitude from a state of isolation and loneliness into a state of grace, solitude becomes the fertile ground from which creative insight springs.

······ ·· ●

Something profoundly sustaining occurs within us when we manage to shut out everything else in order to hold and be held by the object of our focus. In stillness, we ponder the essence of matters that inform our project, distilling fine nuances and shades of meaning that previously escaped our notice. Concentration precedes the click of recognition that announces we have found a direction.

Only through an active and penetrating engagement with ourselves can we discover the source of the creative river. The discipline of concentration allows us to find that flow. Once we break through the surface ripples and refractions, we will discover a torrent of internal suggestions for how to proceed. When standing outside and apart from the river, we feel ignorant, at a loss to begin. Sometimes this illusion of separateness causes us to panic. But if we can just remember to breathe and hold a steady course, we will eventually pass through the layers of restless distraction, we will penetrate the mind chatter and become one with the river. Everything we need to proceed can be found there . . . inside . . . in the mystery of our own unexplored depths.

Further Reflections On Concentration

Thought concentrated for an explicit purpose becomes power! If you wish to go deeper, explore one or more of the following questions. *Write, draw, dance, paint, meditate . . .*

☞ How long can I focus on one thing without interrupting myself to do something else?

☞ When I sit down to concentrate, what happens? What qualities of thought, sensation, and emotion become present in my body?

☞ What conditions in my environment promote my ability to concentrate? What practices, habits, or rituals might help me focus?

☞ What keeps me from focusing on a cherished project, idea, or change I want to make?

☞ Does being alone with my thoughts bring up uncomfortable feelings? Precisely where in my body do I feel them?

☞ When I become distracted, what can I do to refocus?

☞ How far am I willing to go to reduce distractions that prevent me from connecting with the sources of inspiration? What might I need to heal or change in order to improve my ability to concentrate?

☞ Consider the ancient wisdom of Roman philosopher Seneca: "To be everywhere is to be nowhere."

The universe gestures to us all the time. If we learn how to read those gestures, we become more literate, more able to follow the signs that really matter.

—Carlos Castaneda

The real voyage of discovery lies not in seeking new landscapes, but in having new eyes.

—Marcel Proust

There's an art to wandering, to visiting new places with your eyes wide open and your senses alert.

—Petah Coyne

Discovery

ONCE YOU HAVE SOME SENSE of what you're after, it's time to venture out into the world and look. LOOK! And, what do you look for? Everything that might assist you in developing your idea, anything that helps to move the work forward. What do you look with? Your whole body— including your mind, heart, and senses. Where do you look?

E v e r y w h e r e.

When your eyes are wide open inspiration abounds. LOOK! On a bustling street corner or in the hallowed halls of a research library. LOOK! In airports, museums, hardware stores, flea markets, restaurants, shopping malls, and movie theaters. LOOK! During parties, church bazaars, and even funerals. And outdoors along a creekside trail or amid the dark beauty of a starlit night. LOOK!

Don't forget to look in the attic and under the pile of neglected papers stacked in a corner. Look in the scent of a rose and the flight of a hawk. Look with an aching heart in the bitter taste of betrayal, in the whisper of a lover's caress, and in the sound of a baby crying.

Creators look in both familiar and unfamiliar places; they look for the obvious and the obscure. They look deliberately and diligently. And if they look long enough, a propitious grace arrives unbidden. With a focused intention and an open mind, your idea will draw energy to itself. This strange *phenomenon of attraction* can become a creator's most powerful ally.

······`··•

I am nearly halfway through my life before I can find the nerve to share my writing with others. I don't really think of myself as a writer, but I don't want to hide behind a mask of professionalism either. I want my clients to see something of my struggle—and to understand that imperfection lies at the heart of the human condition. The point isn't to fix ourselves. I am certainly not fixed; and my job isn't to fix my clients, although many of them imagine that I will. The point is to stay conscious while making a voyage of discovery into our fallibility.

I don't have any ambitions for my writing beyond sending out my thoughts and feelings in the form of my own quarterly publication. But despite the low bar I set for myself, I still feel incredibly anxious about the prospect of sharing so much of myself so publicly. Yet, it feels important to do it anyway. (Remember, this is decades before social media, networks, and blogging have made the notion of a private life obsolete.)

The sense of excruciating exposure reinforces a daunting awareness of responsibility. *It is all up to me!* I feel totally alone with the commitment I have made. I greet approaching deadlines with panic and crushing self-doubt.

After a while, I begin to observe an interesting pattern of serendipity. Somehow, seemingly by magic, people and things appear in my path as offerings. Even the simple act of opening a book at random and finding the perfect poem or quote hints at something beyond my own conscious efforts. (Is this what author Carlos Castaneda meant when he said, "The universe gestures to us all the time?") Once I recognize and acknowledge the existence of such a benevolent force, I begin to count on its assistance. After a while, I anticipate each issue with less dread and more confidence.

······∙∙●

The essence of discovery lies in trusting your attraction to the odd idea, image, or impulse. A decade after those rocky beginnings, I am waiting to pay for my purchases at a local bookstore when I find myself attracted to a small paperback left on the counter by the person in front of me. Casually flipping through pages, I happen upon the publisher's statement at the back of the book—*we publish books that nourish the hearts and souls of our readers*. In a time-stopping, heart-stopping moment, the words leap from the page to puncture my defenses.

Although I have always been too intimidated to send anything to a publisher, my body shudders in recognition. This is no random encounter: It is another gesture from the Universe, an invitation to take my writing to the next level. The next day, I mail a collection of my personal essays to that publisher. The book you hold in your hand would, most likely, not exist if it weren't for that moment of discovery.

You cannot do everything by yourself. You must take on the challenge and effort of creation, but once you truly commit, *synchronicity* lends you a hand. It's the old adage about chance favoring the prepared mind. If you are not receptive, you will not make the connection. You will walk past whatever discovery has been put in your path without even noticing.

······ ··•

When you open to discovery, you move through the world wide awake. Your receptive presence invites possibility to claim you. Guided by your sense of purpose, acknowledge what catches your attention, make a note of it, and follow up. Sometimes you won't immediately understand why something interests you or where it fits, but don't discount anything too quickly, otherwise you risk short-circuiting the process or creating a poor quality outcome.

Don't lose sight of the joy of discovery by becoming preoccupied with the zealous pursuit of results. Keep in mind that during discovery, you'll want to focus on *gathering information* that will be processed and evaluated at a later stage. It's not always easy, but try to balance discipline and determination with the capacity to have fun and go with the flow.

I know a photographer who drives into the country on weekends, in pursuit of her subject. The theme that informs her search is movement, but she never knows where she will find it or what will catch her attention. Sometimes her camera rests its eye on a farmer's windswept field, at other times it captures a child's midair leap from a backyard swing. She takes hundreds of shots because she cannot know which ones will turn out best.

Photography, like all creative endeavors, involves an act of discovery. If my friend stops to determine the value of each shot prior to clicking the shutter, she risks missing a magical moment. And once the magic of discovery is lost, the process stops being an adventure and starts becoming a self-conscious obsession. Only later will she be able to make sense of the images she has recorded.

You can never predict exactly which piece of information will trigger that essential connection, opening a previously unseen door. For this reason, you need to permit yourself the widest possible latitude during discovery.

·······•

If you want to create, you need to become an explorer. An explorer may be an astronaut living in a space station or a pop songwriter attempting to compose an opera or a former welfare recipient heading off to a first day of work. As an explorer, you must want to find out what lies beyond the boundaries of what you already understand and what you already know how to do. Put yourself in places where you don't know how it's going to work out. Explore the greatest possibilities that you can imagine. Open yourself to choices that don't feel obvious or even natural—that's when you can discover something really interesting.

When I surrender to the creative process, I relish the experience of being on a great adventure—sometimes exhilarating, often profound, always mysterious. At other times, the uncertainty of discovery looms like a menacing force that threatens to swallow me up and destroy my fragile hold on reality. Discovery can be like opening Pandora's box. Let's face it, things don't always work out. You might get lost or discover things aren't quite what you had believed or imagined, and, even more frightening, you may possibly open a door that cannot be closed and you will have to live with the consequences. One thing I can guarantee: Sooner or later the process will take you in whatever direction you have been assiduously avoiding. You can never predict what will happen because the whole point is to explore uncharted territory and create new maps. That is discovery's delight and peril.

Like the courageous explorers that have gone before, you face the prospect of danger and wonder at every turn. New sights, sounds, tastes, and smells. New ideas and feelings. New successes. New disappointments, frustrations, and losses. New choices. Always, another horizon beckons beyond the one you can see. Remember to watch for the signs. *What worlds within and around you await your discovery?*

Further Reflections On Discovery

Discovery consists of looking at the same thing as everyone else and seeing something different. If you wish to go deeper, explore one or more of the following questions. *Write, draw, dance, paint, meditate . . .*

☞ How important are comfort and predictability to my well-being? How might I benefit from cultivating a greater sense of adventure?

☞ How do I feel about taking off without plans or expectations of what I will encounter?

☞ What happened the last time I discovered something unexpected in a situation I thought I had figured out? How did I use that discovery creatively?

☞ When I take a silent walk, what claims my attention?

☞ What places, people, and activities stimulate fresh perspectives?

☞ How does the Universe gesture to me?

*Creative activity could be described as a type of
learning process where teacher and pupil inhabit
the same individual.*

—Arthur Koestler

*I am always doing that which I cannot do, in order
that I may learn how to do it.*

—Pablo Picasso

*You have learned something! That always feels at
first as if you had lost something.*

—George Bernard Shaw

Learning

MOST OF THE ENERGY you will expend over the course of your creative
life involves learning of one sort or another. Creators relish periods of
clarity and productivity, but in between there are even longer phases
of study, practice, questioning, faltering, and groping your way toward
completion. Each time you come up against what feels like a limitation,
the creative process asks that you learn something and then it asks
you to learn something else and before you know it, you find yourself
doing the impossible.

Learning often involves memorizing facts, developing techniques,
or acquiring skills. But, there is learning that goes beyond the practical. There is learning that is deep and lyrical. To be responsive, to
question, to risk exploring all aspects of experience, to seek meaning,
to reach out past the limits of the known, to be changed by what you

have discovered in the world—all of this falls within learning's expansive domain. Learning can be as simple and painless as looking up the name of a bird that sings outside your window or as complex and heartbreaking as realizing that your previous values, goals, and commitments don't matter to you anymore. Whenever new knowledge causes you to question your previous assumptions, the stage is set for creative transformation.

······˙··●

As you embark on the creative path, you will find yourself stepping out into uncharted territory. Without a map, much of the time you navigate in a state of uncertainty, always learning as you go. If you feel uncomfortable or embarrassed by your lack of knowledge, then you will, in all likelihood, give up and retreat to safer ground and familiar competencies. If you have ever wondered whether or not you have what it takes, ask yourself: *Am I really "uncreative" or am I simply uncomfortable with the vulnerability that comes with being a learner?*

The essential challenge of learning is to embrace your ignorance—to see it as the state of mind that inspires exciting adventures in acquiring knowledge and experience. In the creative process, it isn't what you know that counts, but what you don't know. The legendary film director Federico Fellini once remarked on the necessity of not knowing: "I must be ignorant of what I shall be doing . . . I can find the resources I need *only* when I am plunged into obscurity and *ignorance*" (my italics).

Ignorance is not the same thing as stupidity, although the words are often used interchangeably. I often ask my clients: "If you have never done something before—no matter how intelligent you are—does it seem fair to expect yourself to know how to do it, let alone do it well?" Even so, embarrassed clients come to their sessions apologizing for their lack of understanding, as if it were a character defect.

Too many of us feel humiliated when we reach the limits of our knowledge and experience, especially when we must confront the mistakes we may have made out of ignorance. We end up folding in on ourselves, thereby turning away from the possibility of learning. Gradually, we lose the capacity for receptivity.

In the classic book *Zen Mind, Beginner's Mind,* master teacher Shunryu Suzuki calls the quality of mind that is open and available for learning "beginner's mind." In the beginner's mind there are many possibilities. When we assume we should already know everything, we limit our possibilities. If we accept being a beginner—no matter our level of expertise—we release ourselves from the expectation to be strong and in control all the time. We let go of the need to be good at something in order to allow ourselves the freedom to be awkward and unsure—to stumble and fall and to find our feet again. As creators we must grant ourselves the indispensable liberty of celebrating our ignorance in order to go wherever the learning process takes us.

······ ·· ●

In school, we learned to raise our hands, stay in our seats, and not disrupt class. We learned to wait until called on. As creators, this learned passivity does not support our process. We can no longer afford to sit quietly until someone gives us permission to live our dreams.

If you want to flex your creative muscle, you need to take responsibility for your learning process. Ask yourself: *What environments and teaching styles best support my ability to learn?*

Many people do well in structured settings, they thrive on formal instruction, pressure, and competition. Some like to keep moving, learning through their bodies or in cooperation with others. Personally, I like to follow my intuition and work at my own pace. If I have a long-term goal, I generally work the details out as I go along, which means there are long periods where I don't know what I am doing. I need solitude, space, and lots of time. I don't do well under pressure. If I need help, I'd rather receive the undivided attention of a mentor, friend, or private instructor than sit in a classroom.

Remember, there is no right way to learn; what works for others may not work for you. Years ago, several well-meaning friends suggested that in order to write I should take a class or join a writer's group. I tried it for a while, but I felt pressured by that level of structure and critical feedback. Instead, I took on the kind of learning commitment that was right for me.

Most importantly, I didn't try to be a Great Writer.

What I really wanted was to dedicate myself to something larger than myself as a way to recover a sense of wholeness, and the writing process seemed like a good path. It was a matter of giving up trying to control the process and proceeding with an attitude of "What would happen if . . . ?"

My practice was to stick with writing long enough to gradually get better at doing it. But becoming "good" at it wasn't really the point, as it turned out. I kept working with my natural rhythms, and, often, I would set small, achievable goals. But mostly, I let the process draw out deeper levels of character and strength that, in turn, helped me to reach new levels of accomplishment. At the beginning my progress was nearly imperceptible, but after five or six years, I could see that I had improved significantly from where I started.

I had learned something.

Becoming attuned to your own learning process is an art form in itself—one that makes all the difference between attempting to do something and actually doing it.

······•

Creators can expect to feel some emotional discomfort when learning, but too much stress diminishes the mind's capacity to take in anything new. An encouraging attitude combined with an appropriate level of difficulty empowers you to create. Balance the challenge of extending your boundaries with the safety of rest and retreat. Stepping back after periods of intense learning facilitates integration and absorption of new knowledge. However, if you find yourself languishing, you may not be demanding enough of yourself. To make learning enjoyable, find an acceptable trade-off between feeling you're in control of things and feeling vulnerable.

Learning is never what we anticipate. We want it to be easy and it is not. Beset by contradictory thoughts and feelings, we find our-selves questioning whether the creative journey is worth the effort. Despite our uncertainty, we must take the next step in learning. And then the next.

The frustration, tension—and yes, the many failures that precede mastery—help creators acquire new skills and wisdom. Just on the other side of struggle, just beyond the point where you want to give up—a door opens. And suddenly, everything that seemed in conflict finds a way to come together. You feel stronger, your intention is clearer. You have broken through the impasse and can bask in sanguine anticipation of what is yet to come. Learning has renewed your spirit.

Further Reflections On Learning

Learning involves the freedom to struggle, to make mistakes, to ask questions—even the same questions—again and again. If you wish to go deeper, explore one or more of the following questions. *Write, draw, dance, paint, meditate . . .*

☛ How do I keep learning and growing as a creator? What excites me?

☛ How well do I tolerate the frustration and incompetence that generally precede mastery? Can I bounce back from mistakes and setbacks?

☛ Do I prefer learning in a nurturing, cooperative environment, a driven, competitive environment, or do I prefer learning things on my own?

☛ Where have I given up on myself too soon because of the challenge of learning? Reflecting on this decision, how do I feel about myself? What actions can I take in the future to develop resilience, grit, and optimism when confronting the challenge of learning?

☛ Closing my eyes: Where in my body can I still feel the wounds from early encounters with learning? What happened? What new directions might open up provided I give myself permission to be a learner?

☛ Reflecting on any regrets I may have, what have I learned? What would I like to do differently?

☛ What do I need to learn in order to do the thing that really matters to me?

☛ When learning, how can celebrating the small victories help me accomplish the larger ones?

As for myself, I experience a sort of terror when, at the moment of setting to work and finding myself before the infinitude of possibilities that present themselves, I have the feeling that everything is permissible to me.

—Igor Stravinsky

Anything you build with passion invites chaos.

—Francis Ford Coppola

In chaos, there is fertility.

—Anaïs Nin

Chaos

HOW SHALL I BEGIN? *Fragments of thought and feeling whirl around competing for my attention: ≈Head Swirls≈ ≈Stomach Swirls≈ Will this idea work? What if it doesn't? Uh-Oh. . .Memoryfloodingexample Examples? Slow down. . .Too Fast. Which one? Where does Bob go? Page what? Change that!No leave it! Where did I put that quote? How's this: Chaos is present whenever there is outward expansion. Yes I like it! <Heart Beating Faster> Let's start<<Try It>> Doesn't really work. <Back Stiffens> OK. Breathe>TrySomething Else.>Breathe>Breathe>Breathein-to<thesoundofthedistantwind>*

 Begin Again.

As we set out to explore the various possibilities for an idea, everything that we are learning will eventually extend our knowledge beyond the horizons of our neatly ordered world. When the creative process takes us past the ability to keep track of things, the boundaries of the familiar collapse into chaos. Only a very few creators actually relish this scary and stomach-churning state. The rest of us have to learn how to channel its power.

Gathering multiple sources of information during the learning and discovery phases of the creative process naturally results in chaos. At some point, the mind and senses become overstimulated by processing so much new input; we begin to experience the dizzying effects of perceptual overload. Everything we consider seems to take on a life of its own, swirling around in an apparently unconnected fashion. Nothing makes any sense.

······ ···•

Once we have entered the engulfing whirl of chaos, we no longer have control. At such disquieting times, we may forget the vital role chaos plays in stimulating leaps of insight. My client, Bob, is a CEO who channels the energy of chaos much like an artist: He doesn't necessarily like it, but he doesn't fight it either. When looking for solutions to the complex challenges of running a large financial institution, Bob tells me: "I need to stay overwhelmed for as long as possible while trying to understand the problem at deeper and deeper levels." Staying engaged with chaos is the key: "*That's where the ideas come from*," he emphasizes. "It's overwhelming, frustrating, even a little sad because the old solutions aren't working any more, but the very thing that feels so scary also holds the promise for a better way."

During our conversation, Bob likens his mental confusion to entering a maze. "You go into it numerous times and each time you wander around blindly before finally coming out in a different place, with a different idea to try. There are always multiple answers. Even after I think I have found the optimum solution, all I can do is implement it for a while and get feedback."

"What if it doesn't work?" I inquire. Bob shakes his head resignedly, "I just have to go back into the maze of confusion again—I don't necessarily get it right the first time." Laughing, he concludes, "Of course, that's really hard because I don't like the discomfort of feeling uncertain and of having to admit that the answer I thought I had found just isn't all that I had hoped for."

As Bob so vividly points out, learning to respect the process of groping amidst a whirlpool of sensation and ideas can be challenging. Imposing your will on a situation, forcing things to connect too soon, may bring immediate relief from the discomfort of intellectual chaos, but answers arrived at in this fashion will ultimately inhibit the flow of vibrant energy required to keep the project moving in the direction of the highest quality outcome.

······•

In the natural world, we witness nature's cycles of chaos and order as life continuously struggles to renew itself. So too in our own lives. Without the fresh connections made possible by the disruption of comfortable and established patterns, nothing new can be created. Even if you are the most ardent control freak, you can learn to become more comfortable with the energy of chaos by taking care of yourself when you feel overwhelmed.

Self-nurturing activities that center, nourish, and support creators in their work include meditation, walking, gardening, listening to music, knitting, hot baths, playing with children, intimate conversation with a friend, dancing, visiting galleries or museums, relaxing on a park bench, being on or near the water, running along a mountain trail, watching a sunrise or sunset, lifting weights, chopping vegetables for a salad, and organizing the garage or studio. Take a moment to reflect: *What are my own practices for coming back to myself? Is there something on this list that might work for me?*

When stressed and scared, you may be tempted to indulge impulsive options that provide momentary comfort but leave you feeling guilty, hung over, in debt, or too distressed to stay engaged. Make sure your choices do not simply distract or obscure the discomfort of chaos—they need to leave you feeling refreshed, empowered, and receptive to whatever wants to communicate with you from the depths.

·······•

In a creative life we must remain open to the *shadow side*, those aspects of ourselves and our life experience we'd just as soon not confront. We must also remain open to the strange worlds beyond everyday reality. Inspired creators strive to know things in their deepest sense—to see what lies beyond form. Traditional cultures have always acknowledged and revered the role of chaos as the gateway to other sacred realities: fertility and the realm of the sensual as well as healing wisdom and intuitive understanding beyond anything the rational mind can fathom.

A master teacher, chaos disrupts complacency while bringing attention to skills and possibilities that lie outside of conscious awareness. Whether we are knocked off balance by something unforeseen or we consciously step over our own barriers to become something new, chaos helps us discover there is far more to us than we know—there exists a depth of insight and capacity that has previously escaped our notice. For open-minded creators, the power of chaos reveals invisible truth, announcing the coming of something great but as yet unseen.

Further Reflections On Chaos

The turmoil that accompanies creative chaos ushers in fresh new realities. If you wish to go deeper, explore one or more of the following questions. *Write, draw, dance, paint, meditate . . .*

➤ Amid chaos, what kinds of sensations do I experience in my body?

➤ How do I currently care for myself during the physical and psychological stress of creative chaos?

➤ What do I need so that I might feel more genuinely nourished in my creative life?

➤ Recalling times when I have weathered the storm of chaos, how did I manage? How was I able to reinvent myself as a result? What lessons can I apply to my current situation?

➤ What deeper patterns remain a constant in my life no matter how much things change? In what ways can I allow myself to feel supported by them?

Concerning all acts of creation, there is one elementary
truth: the moment one definitely commits oneself, then
Providence moves too.

—W. H. Murray

[Creators] commit themselves to the work of their
heart and act upon that commitment.

—David Bayles & Ted Orland

Commitment can be a duty; it can be love; it can
flow naturally; it can be a hard-fought act of will . . .
a pledge to the work rooted in the deeper authority of self.

—Eric Maisel

Commitment

CREATIVITY REQUIRES A DEEP, intense connection between yourself and
what you bring into being. Whether writing a novel, composing a
symphony, throwing a pot, or starting a business, you are not simply
producing a *thing*; you are in relationship with something vital, which
has a spirit of its own. When first getting started, you will find many
reasons to quit. Through commitment, you promise to work from start
to finish with whatever arises on the journey, however difficult and
discouraging. And like any committed relationship, your project has
the potential to bring out both the best and the worst in you.

When we create from our heart's desire, something powerful and
authentic awakens deep inside. The experience feels a lot like falling in
love. *Remember those invigorating feelings that open our hearts and minds
to the possibility for reinvention?* We make hopeful promises: "It will be

different this time." But like the early stages of a romance, euphoria eventually gives way to the reality of issues, conflict, and negotiation.

The creative process follows a similar path. When the heart awakens, so do the slumbering dragons (who are none too happy about having their beauty sleep disturbed). Once the initial excitement of getting started fades, we must face the reality of what we have taken on: "OMG! What have I done?!!"

Furious doubts and hidden fears emerge from hibernation, and their combined weight can block the flow of inspiration. In the absence of genuine commitment, we may simply blow away when the first storm hits. For many, just making the decision to commit is half the battle.

······⋯•

Unless we understand our issues surrounding commitment, we may spend years making excuses, collapsing, or running in the face of creative opportunity. My client Craig has done precisely that. For more than twenty years, he has started and abandoned a number of projects, all of which sounded promising.

"In the beginning," Craig tells me, "I always feel excited and hopeful because the goal seems to be within my grasp."

But as obstacles arise, he reports that his sense of excitement deflates into disheartening doubt and pessimism, leading him to abandon his efforts. I ask Craig if he has any idea why he becomes so discouraged. "I never thought about it before, but I guess I feel sort of trapped—I start wondering whether there's something *better* I could be doing."

Once the initial period of infatuation fades, Craig finds he lacks the internal conviction to continue. He rationalizes his decisions to quit by telling himself that he just hasn't found "it" yet. But the obstacle blocking Craig's creative path does not lie in the outside world. He doesn't need to find the perfect project—*Craig needs to say yes and mean it.* He sabotages or fails to recognize some good opportunities simply because he can't cope with the feelings that arise whenever he contemplates closing off his options. He fails to persevere because he refuses to commit.

·······•

Many people who have difficulty with commitment find themselves seduced by the illusion of possibility and freedom—the kind of freedom where we can just pack up whenever life's disappointments and demands start to close in too tightly. I call this the Dream of Opportunity and Second Chances. While *dreams* inspire and uplift the spirit, *commitment* sinks deep roots into the soul, securing the ground for follow-through and completion. Absent commitment, we risk losing ourselves in a perpetual horizontal journey to nowhere. Commitment-phobes frequently replace one dream with a different dream or one circumstance with another, not because the other option has more veracity, not for the sake of making a contribution, but simply for the sake of something new.

I can empathize with Craig's dilemma because I also spent many years following freedom's call over and over again. One day, I woke up and realized that I had nothing to show for all this liberty except a trail of wrong turns and false hopes. Somewhere along the way, without even realizing it, my youthful experimentation had crossed the line from self-discovery into abandonment of self.

Eventually, I stopped moving from option to option. I finally had to make a choice and stick with it. It was an important lesson: All creative opportunities involve problems and all problems give rise to creative opportunities. Sometimes there isn't something better, if *better* secretly means *easier*.

Once I stood my ground, I discovered another sort of latitude—the kind that can only be found within the structure of limits. *Fertile limits.*

Real freedom begins when you give yourself permission to succeed at whatever has meaning for you—*and find a way to do it.*

Fertile limits become the boundaries within which your creativity can flourish. These limits take the creative journey in a vertical direction by empowering you to dig more deeply into yourself so you can convert personal limitations into assets while discovering capacities you didn't realize you had. Sometimes creators freely choose their *fertile limits,* such as when consciously retreating from tempting distractions in order to finish a project. At other times, creators face inherent limitations, accidents of nature and biology.

The poet Emily Dickinson spent years hiding in her house. Was she suffering from the psychological disorder agoraphobia? Probably. But within the confines of her fear and the room she rarely left, she wrote some of the world's most emotionally affecting poetry. Her need to withdraw became the *fertile limit* that gave her the space and time to write poetry. The painter Chuck Close credits his neurological disabilities with helping him choose art over academics. A self-confessed "terrible test taker," he had such a bad memory that he could only remember a face by breaking it down into small "bite-sized" pieces—just like the tiny circles or squares that eventually made up his prints and paintings. "I figured out what I had left and tried to make it work for me," he said. Whatever their source, a creator's limitations, however personally painful—and a commitment to capitalize on those limitations—help drive the creative journey.

Begin exploring your *fertile limits* by asking yourself: *What makes me different? Where do I fall short? What challenges and circumstances do I habitually avoid? What fear or other sensitivity might be trying to point the way toward a unique destiny?*

······ˈ··●

When we finally do commit to closing off the exits, that's when the process really starts to get interesting. We begin to notice that everything else leaves. All the "buts," all the excuses—all the emotional dramas, all the whining, blaming, and complaining—just drop away and finally we are *free*. At last, we have the freedom to do what it takes to make the project work.

Naturally, within the context of our promises, we must do things that we don't necessarily want to do—we must make sacrifices. We make them willingly, not necessarily easily, because they are in service to what matters deeply. As much as I dread appearing in public, I will need to return to the public stage in order to help *Wild Ideas* get noticed. So even though I have terrible stage fright, even though I would rather hang by my toes than stand in front of an audience—I will do it! I will do the book tours, make presentations, show up for interviews. I will do all that and more because I believe in my book and want it to find a home in the hearts and minds of a wide audience. *Love transforms sacrifice from a burden into an offering.* We commit to nourishing our creations—like our children—through all the stages of their lives, even the difficult ones.

······∙•

As we gain insight into ourselves and our motivations, the path becomes clearer. We begin to see it in a hundred different places. More and more, we recognize a strong and solid feeling emerging from within as our passion takes root and moves us toward a unique destiny.

Commitment comes little by little. We need to say yes to our dreams many times. Always, we must be mindful of the impulse for distraction and dissolution. We work, we doubt, we procrastinate, we work again. We may leave, and then, when we miss the work, struggle back to it. As we deepen within the work, the cycle repeats itself. Years may pass.

If we are lucky, we may learn that we cannot thrive without the work. If we discover—through all the enduring—that nothing else quite delights us, nourishes us, expands us or—dare I say—loves us, then commitment to the work becomes a joy and a necessity.

Further Reflections On Commitment

All meaningful commitments ask you to confront your fears. If you wish to go deeper, explore one or more of the following questions. *Write, draw, dance, paint, meditate . . .*

☞ What am I committed to creating in my life?

☞ When I think about this commitment how does my body feel? Why is it important to me?

☞ Creators must sometimes say *no* to something that matters in order to say *yes* to what matters more. Can I say no? Am I overcommitted to things that leave me feeling exhausted and depleted? What do I need to release in order to bring about my vision?

☞ What calls to me over and over even though I keep walking away? What scares me about answering the call?

☞ Can I say *yes* and mean it? Is is natural for me to give my all? If I do tend to hold something in reserve, why do I hold back?

☞ How do my past experiences inform my commitments today? What might I need to heal so I can strengthen my capacity for commitment.

☞ What makes me different? How might I amplify and channel my *fertile limits* into creative work?

☞ If I am currently considering a commitment, does it align with my passion and purpose? Who will benefit? What resources do I need? What might go wrong so I can plan ahead?

☞ How can I prepare for those inevitable times when I feel disheartened, unmotivated, and insignificant?

☞ How will I stay connected when I most want to flee? What resources can I put into place NOW—before I lose heart—to help me stay committed to my work?

Every beginning is a promise
born in light and dying . . .

—*Brendan Kennelly*

We're all the same really, we just get stuck in different ways.

—Pema Chödrön

A blocked path also offers guidance.

—Mason Cooley

To find an opening one has to make a breach in the wall—and the wall is almost always in one's own mind.

—Henry Miller

3

Hitting the Wall

SO MANY THINGS ABOUT the creative process are difficult or scary or downright painful. Or simply don't turn out the way we would like them to. Creators may find themselves hitting a wall at any time during the creative process. Some are passionately inspired but can't focus their restless energy in order to begin. Others begin successfully but get stuck in the middle of their own personal no man's land—too far from home but nowhere near the destination. Many run the race, but stop just short of crossing the finish line, daunted by the consequences of completion. While others, too shy or intimidated by the demands of feedback, retreat from the pressures of taking their creations public. Ask yourself: *Which stages of the creative process challenge me the most?*

Creativity involves a natural ebb and flow of productivity for a variety of reasons. Sometimes when we are trying to do something prematurely, it just won't come. In such instances, feeling blocked isn't really a barrier at all, but merely a sign to back away from the problem for a while. At other times, creators hit the wall because of deep-rooted conflicts. Unremitting stuckness may be a cry for help. Left unattended, unresolved life experiences can disrupt a creator's focus, eventually disabling motivation altogether. Ask yourself: *Am I stuck?*

As a creator, you must become wise to the ways you stop yourself—since the wall is almost always erected by your own insecurities. You must open a window in the wall—a way to see into your frightened mind. You open that window by acknowledging, embracing, and expressing the insecurities on the other side. Ask yourself: *Am I ready to free myself?*

We restore the flow of creative energy by opening our minds and hearts, by receiving with love and understanding those banished aspects of ourselves—the confusing, the frightening, the painful, and yes, even the joyful. In the absence of self-awareness, too many creators become their own worst enemy, sabotaging rather than supporting their dreams. Ask yourself: *If I didn't feel stuck right now what might I have to feel, think about, or confront?*

Hitting the wall signals an opportunity for revelation and recovery. Dreams that once seemed out of reach become achievable in the context of our healing process. When we feel stuck, we stop. And in that soulful silence, we have a chance to retrieve a part of ourselves that has been forced into exile. We have a chance to find out, perhaps for the first time, who we really are.

Qualities that challenge creators and nourish creative growth include *problems, resistance, suffering, compassion,* and *courage.*

Problems test us, helping to develop skills, confidence, and character, while infusing our lives with a sense of adventure and meaning. *Resistance* tries to block the pain associated with facing problems and dealing with change. *Suffering* and sacrifice prepare us to receive creative blessings. *Compassion* softens the heart and attends to creative suffering. *Courage* provides the strength and determination to find a way through.

The meaning and purpose of a problem seems to lie not in its solution but in our working at it incessantly. This alone preserves us against stultification and petrification.

—Carl Jung

Every creative journey begins with a problem. It starts with a feeling of frustration, the dull ache of not being able to find the answer.

—Jonah Lehrer

You're either going to have the problems that come with realizing this vision of your's, or the neurotic problems that arise from the suppression of desire.

—Lauren G. Boldt

Problems

AT THE HEART OF THE CREATIVE PROCESS lies a problem waiting to be solved. The problem might be as modest as how to paint the beauty of a flower, as grand as finding a cure for cancer, or as personal as how to leave an abusive relationship. A creator asks three questions: *What is the nature of the problem? Can it be done? Can I do it?* Whether we respond thoughtfully or react unconsciously defines the outcome as creative or merely expedient.

The process of engaging and solving problems gives life meaning. Honestly, I know this to be true. But when I was given the opportunity to write this book, everything I thought I had learned and lived about creative problem solving went the way of the dodo bird.

At least at first . . .

When I find out that I will be embarking on a book-writing

adventure, I feel terribly excited about the possibilities—for about two hours. I call everyone I know to tell them of my good fortune—that a small publisher has asked me to write a book about creativity. ME! It all seems positively surreal. I soar in a kind of waking dream, flying around on cloud nine or ten when it suddenly dawns on me that this incredible opportunity I have been given is also a BIG problem for me to solve—a problem I have spent decades avoiding.

Although I have been writing much of my adult life, I've kept my writing practice simple and manageable. Hovering between 800 and 1500 words, the short essay as a column is something I understand and—most important—something I can confidently start and finish. So naturally, at the first meeting to discuss the project, my comfort zone takes a direct hit: "We need three hundred pages by spring." Watching the editor's lips move, I nod complacently in apparent agreement while a voice in my head screams: THREE HUNDRED PAGES!!!

He might as well have said three thousand.

······ ···●

How in the world will I ever find the discipline and endurance to complete such an enormous task?

Before I have a chance to think about how I might solve this glorious problem, waves of anxiety, doubt, helplessness, and paralysis sweep over me.

At this point, disbelieving but excited me—"You actually asked me, ME!!!"—unceremoniously dissolves into whining me—"Whyymeee!"

Seized by a sudden terror, my mind races light years into the future, where I see a vision of myself as an old woman, marooned on an island with only my half-finished book for a companion. Then I take an abrupt U-turn into the distant past where memories of wasted chances replay themselves over and over.

It's all very disconcerting.

I've been handed a wonderful challenge. An opportunity to fulfill a secret dream! Not a bad problem to have, as far as problems go. But my mind is so busy time traveling that there really isn't a whole lot of room to think about how I will go about meeting this challenge.

Days later, I finally land back in the here and now.

I realize that the challenges inherent in writing a book will be daunting. But the more fundamental problem, the problem that could sabotage my ability to write at all is *the problem of my own character.* My reluctance to engage with the ongoing demands, responsibilities, and sacrifices inherent in any long-term problem-solving venture has dogged my highly sensitive, free-spirited nature throughout my life and will surely threaten to undo me once again.

Still, I recognize a propitious moment.

(Not just the lurking dangers.)

I will not let it pass without at least making the effort.

······⋯•

I wake up in fear every day. I will myself to go into my office and turn on the computer anyway. After I read what I wrote the day before, I tell myself to focus on the chapter, the section, the page, the paragraph, the sentence directly in front of me. And in the instant that I begin to work on the problem, my fear dissolves.

Sometimes, all we need as creators is a moment of grace.

Despite my anxiety, another day's work manages to complete itself. Before long, I find myself accomplishing the real work of problem-solving: finding a way to show up each day despite palpable and sometimes overwhelming doubt and fear. Just doing the work, even badly, helps me bump into something useful. "Inspiration exists," says Pablo Picasso, "but it has to find you working."

The feeling of pride mixed with relief mixed with excitement borders on the indescribable.

DELICIOUS.

I am less afraid.

·····∙··●

Once you open the door to desire, a horde of difficulties come galloping out to greet you. If you prefer a life free of complications, avoid the creative path. However, if you want to feel invigorated by the quest, if you value new knowledge and an awakened spirit, then you will welcome the responsibility and exertion involved in grappling with problems.

So what kinds of creative problems might you face? Such problems include all the perplexing questions you encounter in the process of executing your vision.

For example, let's say you want to create a quilt. (Yeah, I don't quilt either, but you'll get the idea.)

First, there's the problem of deciding on the quilt's purpose. Do you plan to use it as a wall hanging, a baby gift, or something else entirely? Questions about design, size, filling, fabric and where to find these materials immediately follow. Will you create your own design or use a traditional one? How much will it all cost and can you afford it? Will you go to the extra trouble of pre-washing and starching the fabric? What about sewing techniques? Will it be hand sewn or machine sewn or some combination of the two? Do you need to learn something new in order to execute the project? If so, where will you get help? What about equipment like a sewing machine, rotary cutter, mat, templates, scissors, thimble, needles, and thread? And if you intend to show or sell your quilt then you will need to find a gallery or some other venue. How will you attract potential buyers? What price should you put on your efforts? And if you also work forty hours a week and raise children, where will you find the time and space to do all this? What if you do make the time, but your family and friends resent your absence?

In the process of addressing these problems, you will inevitably create or discover even more problems.

Perhaps you will uncover a long-forgotten memory of your grand-mother's prize-winning quilts. But that innocent reminiscence threatens to devour your initiative because you think, "Mine will never be as good." Or while shopping for fabric, you find yourself drawn to something really unusual but can't decide whether to take the plunge because you fear it won't work. Or you get started and seem to be progressing quite well when, midway through, you discover that the pattern has been laid out incorrectly and you have to either undo months of stitching or let the mistakes dictate a new course. And don't forget about the problem of detachment and letting go. How will you deal with the heartbreak of watching your lovingly hand-stitched wall hanging slowly fade in the entry way of your best friend's home because she hung it—against your advice—directly in front of a UV light source?

Phew! That's a lot to think about all at once, even if you are a big picture sort of person. Personally, I need to break things down into small, manageable tasks, focusing on one thing at a time. (Whoever conducted the famous study that concluded women are natural mul-titaskers never interviewed me.) Also, I try not to fixate on anything too far ahead. Accomplishing one thing at a time leaves me feeling more confident, less overwhelmed—and ready to take the next step.

Find your own rhythm, keep your own pace, and trust your gut. Above all, take care of yourself. Executing a vision is never easy. Don't let the inevitable problems run you into the ground. Ask yourself: *How do I tackle creative problems? Am I methodical, intuitive, or do I thrive in chaos?*

·····‥·●

It can be helpful to reframe the problems that arise during the creative process as *fertile predicaments*—meaning any quandary that is rich with possibility. Wrestling with our fertile predicaments teaches us about the importance of simply showing up. From the outside, a seemingly impenetrable quandary seems solid and unyielding. However, the moment we step into the fray, the moment we turn to engage whatever we have been avoiding, the problem almost always becomes less intimidating.

When I speak about "wrestling," I am not suggesting that we treat our dilemmas as if they were the enemy. Unconsciously, many of us approach problems from the masculine ideal of conquest. Problems do not appreciate being the target of our stockpile of unresolved feelings of hostility and fear. The drive to conquer a problem in order to force a perfect solution seeks the elimination of snags, difficulties, and complexity—the vital sparks of creation.

Instead of steeling ourselves to do battle, instead of charging in with guns blazing, replace this adversarial approach with a creative one. Strive to form a kind of *partnership* with the problem by cultivating an attitude of receptivity and relatedness. *What do you want? What do I need to do or learn next?*—these are the kinds of questions that open communication between you and the difficulty at hand.

Looking at the problem-solving process as a *partnership* encourages creative solutions. Once we recognize that everything we need to solve the problem comes from our willingness to engage the problem, the problem becomes an ally rather than an adversary.

If we can accept that the problem itself contains suggestions on how it wants to be handled, and if we are focused enough and imaginative enough and sensitive enough, we can glean solutions through an intuitive process of give and take. Answers arrived at in this manner will register first in the body; only later will they be understood, accepted, and fine-tuned by the conscious mind. During the creative process, creators discover splendid problems and give themselves over—body and soul—to exploring their secrets.

Further Reflections on Problems

Whatever you do, there will always be problems that tempt you to believe your doubts and fears are right. If you wish to go deeper, explore one or more of the following questions. *Write, draw, dance, paint, meditate . . .*

☞ What challenge or creative problem am I currently facing?

☞ Does my attitude make the problem worse or better? (Do I take responsibility, trusting the process and my own capabilities? Do I play the victim, waiting for rescue, blaming others or myself, or do I wish my problem would just go away? Do I ignore or procrastinate, fearing the pain that comes with engaging difficulty?)

☞ What is my problem-solving style? (Do I work more efficiently if I compartmentalize, or do I thrive in the chaos? Do I engage the problem and find the resources I need? Do I resist cutting my losses, holding on too long to a strategy that isn't working, or do I give up too easily?) What are the results?

☞ What preconceived ideas do I have about the problem that could be holding me back? How might I reframe the problem from a different perspective? What new possibilities emerge?

☞ Can I recall a similar problem that turned into an opportunity? What strengths did I use to transform the situation? How might I apply these skills and lessons today?

☞ What opportunities lie hidden within the problem, provided I am willing to rise to the challenge? What resources have I not yet considered that may be helpful?

☞ If I close my eyes and visualize putting forth my best effort, what sensations do I feel? How might I express this experience creatively?

☞ If I imagine the problem speaking to me, what does it advise? What do I need to do to achieve the results I seek?

*Only let a man say that he will do something and a
whole mechanism goes to work to stop him.*

—John Steinbeck

*There is a natural tendency to resist the call and hold
fast to the security and predictability of the known.*

—Muriel James

*Finally, on my way to yes, I bump into the places
where I say no . . .*

—Pesha Gerber

Resistance

DO YOU KNOW ANYONE who has anything good to say about their
problems? Most of us do not welcome problems as invited guests. In
fact, we form bonds of friendship by taking turns complaining about
our problems. When was the last time you called up a friend to say,
"Hi, you won't believe what a fantastic problem I have—I get to be
creative today!" We so rarely want to be associated with problems that
we look for ways to push them off onto other people. "Hey, this isn't my
problem, it's yours. Here, take it. It's not my fault."

But really, who can blame us? Problems behave badly, barging in
without calling first and expecting us to drop everything to accom-
modate their every need, or worse, to change our lives around just
to suit them. What nerve. Even when we anticipate their arrival, no
matter how much we prepare in advance, they still seem to require too

much of our time and attention. We have a life to live, after all. Darn those pesky problems and their terrible sense of timing. What's a poor, beleaguered host or hostess to do but bar the door and pretend no one is home?

The problem with problems is that they ask us to make changes and take responsibility. And change and responsibility can be darned uncomfortable. Since creators tackle problems other people don't want to deal with, we're going to be riding the waves of change and its attendant discomforts practically all the time.

All human beings, even creative ones, have been hardwired by nature to resist the discomfort of change. *The powerful instinct of resistance protects us from the threat of pain.* Unfortunately, this instinct is not particularly astute. It can't distinguish pain that inspires ingenuity from pain that foreshadows affliction and apocalypse. Armed with a seemingly unlimited arsenal of tricks, resistance vigilantly pursues its mission to distract, deny, distort, diminish, and divert pain for the sake of our survival. But the regressive tactics employed by resistance frequently become a problem for creators who wish to play at the edge of their limitations.

Strategies for avoiding discomfort frequently backfire and create even more of it. Resistance may present as self-doubt, laziness, grandiosity, self-sabotage, procrastination, negativity, addictions, or other inner demons of various sorts. Even somatic aches and complaints such as fatigue, anxiety, digestive disorders, depression, insomnia, irritability can be signs of resistance doing its job: keeping you safe but frustrating your creativity.

Creative problems are particularly vulnerable to the threat of resistance. Whenever we work creatively, we chase after a dream. And anytime we pursue anything that truly engages our heart at a core level—any long-term goal that involves personal development or self-improvement—we put forth our highest self, delaying gratification in the process while trying to grow beyond the boundaries of the status quo. Resistance tries to preserve these old boundaries for the sake of consistency and continuity. As consciously evolving creators, we need to get out of our own way when the necessity for change must trump the instinct to resist it.

······ ·· ●

The best time to work may be when you resist working the most. If you can circumvent a pattern of refusal, even for a moment, you may find that some of your best work—or at least something new and interesting—breaks through from just beneath the surface.

For many years, I commuted to the county art museum for an after-hours life-drawing group. The weekly sessions ran until late at night. At precisely the midway point, my mind would habitually lose focus and begin anticipating the long drive home. Once my mind took me out of the room, my body sank, awash with fatigue, and my fatigue became an excuse to stop working. I never once stayed for an entire session.

Until one evening . . .

As I begin to gather my drawings, a woman working next to me whispers, "Why don't you stay and stick it out a little longer? You never know what you may discover."

I wince at the implication: Her discreet suggestion reveals my guilty conscience. Reluctantly, I stay—even though I suddenly feel so exhausted I can barely stay on my feet.

At first, it feels physically uncomfortable to work through the fatigue that has always driven me from the demands of the room. Without being able to muster the level of focus I usually maintain, I feel out of sorts. Fuzzy. I am also irritated at myself for letting someone talk me into something I didn't want to do. But I just go along with what feels like sloppy, irritable energy. I keep working, but I also keep fighting the whole idea of staying.

Gradually, the energy of conflict dissipates and something different begins to emerge. I start grabbing colors from my pastel box that I don't normally use—like lime green and neon orange—and my figures become more oddly conformed than usual. I *think*: "This looks really ugly." (At the same time, I *feel* strangely liberated.) Ignoring my judgmental thoughts, I relish the new sensations. Amazingly, I feel like a kid again. The weariness dissipates as my body becomes energized by a zany eccentric that has been hiding beneath my fatigue.

With the memories of artistic failure still as fresh as they were in junior high, just getting to those weekly drawing sessions was a huge stretch. Looking back now, I realized fatigue was how my ambivalence expressed itself. By gently challenging a long-standing habit, I transformed my resistance from a saboteur into a gateway. Ask yourself: *What small step can I take to challenge a long-standing pattern of refusal?*

·····⸱··●

Resistance is a fact of life, so avoid getting into a battle. You can't win. In fact, resistance will cleverly lure you into a power struggle as a way to keep you distracted, defeated, and drifting in circles indefinitely.

Resistance psychology lies behind yo-yo dieting and the perennial making and breaking of New Year's resolutions. Most of us have tried to give up a bad habit or start a healthy one. We begin with good intentions but then, after a period of time, we falter and eventually find reasons to quit. Guilt and disappointment haunt us until, through the magic of resistance, we forget all about it (denial) or find ways to let ourselves off the hook (indulgence and justification). Many of us spend years stuck in these self-defeating cycles.

I once had a client who told me she finally decided to reach out for help after watching herself find excuses not to go into her studio for seventy-five days in a row. "At first, I told myself, 'It's no big deal. I just finished a big show. I'm tired, I deserve a break.' It seemed OK. But then, one day led to another and another. I *couldn't* go back to work. I would wake up and walk toward the studio and then something would stop me, and I found myself organizing my sock drawer or whatever. It's horrifying and fascinating at the same time."

Whenever you find yourself hitting a wall, whether in a creative project or in your life, it's a good bet that resistance is the force sapping your creative energy. Every one of my clients who feels stuck has actually been trapped by a long-standing pattern of resistance that won't allow the *necessary* suffering that the creative process requires. As my client Roy remarked the other day: "It hurts so much to have to see what I have been doing to myself for so long, but it hurts me even more when I keep doing the same old thing over and over. I'm ready to do whatever it takes."

······⋅·⋅●

Resistance draws power from your reluctance to confront it. Recognizing resistance can be frustrating at first. But if you pay attention, you can get better at tracking its surreptitious movements. Start by acknowledging the valuable service resistance has performed for you over the years. Ask yourself: *How has resistance protected me?*

Here are some questions to consider as you reflect. Focus on one or two that speak to your style of resistance, or consider one of your own.

Does procrastination keep me from having to face an uncertain outcome? Does giving up in the middle of a project save me from feeling trapped by commitment or exposed to ridicule? Is it easier to languish within the gray safety of sadness than risk trying again? Do the quantifiable rewards of completing practical tasks make me feel more productive than sitting for hours at my easel and coming away with an ambiguous, subjective result? Does working at a job I hate protect me from the possibility of failing at something I love? Does logging hours of Internet time or partying with friends each weekend feel less lonely than facing the blank walls of my studio? Does drinking soften the edges of a searing sense of inadequacy? Does obsessive worry or complaining protect me from utilizing reserves of deep strength that might compel me to change my life? Is relentless self-criticism gratifying a hidden need to feel powerful? Does not choosing save me from the consequences of choosing wrong?

And that's only the tip of the iceberg. There are so many ways to say *No!*—to ourselves, to our work, to life itself. Regardless of how varied and pervasive your resistance seems to be, *awareness and curiosity are your greatest allies in managing resistance.* When we negotiate with resistance, we have a better chance of moving our dreams forward: "*Hi. I see that you're wanting some attention today. What's up?*"

Help yourself get moving again by attending to the issues that inspire your reluctance. When you ignore, deny, avoid, or buy into the excuses that resistance conjures, you will inevitably remain stuck. Remember to be kind to yourself when tracking and exploring reluctance. Attempts to bully yourself through an impasse may work in the short run, but treating yourself badly will only strengthen your resistance over time. Ask yourself: *What am I afraid of? What might happen if I let myself move forward? Why is the status quo so appealing? What can I do to help myself take the next step?*

······ ·· ●

We tend to throw up roadblocks wherever apprehension, uncertainty, and sacrifice threaten to overwhelm us. Oddly enough, we also resist the *best* in ourselves—the force of our passion, the excitement of inspiration, and the sense of possibility that accompanies the flow of creative energy.

Many of my clients are so convinced that they have nothing to offer that they actually panic when they discover that they do. The prospect of creative abundance can be particularly intimidating if we have lived a previously diminished or depressed existence. In such cases, we may suspiciously greet the arrival of exuberant energy: *This is too good to be true. It probably won't last. I don't deserve this. What's the catch?* Staying open to the creative process means traversing the edge between possibility and loss. Getting knocked on our butt or dragged into the undertow after riding waves of hopeful anticipation can be painful—even devastating. Resistance helps us avoid the ride altogether and spare ourselves the discomfort of all that emotional turmoil.

During one of her sessions, Sheri experiences a powerful awareness of her innate competence. We both agree she's had a real breakthrough. The resulting surge of well-being sparks a new level of vitality and easy productivity which continues unabated for many weeks. One afternoon, Sheri walks through the door and announces, "I really don't think I can take *it* much longer."

"Take *what* much longer?" I inquire.

"It's the tension of waiting for the bough to break," she explains. "I'm starting to feel those little chinks of wanting to beat myself up again. You know . . ."—she hesitates briefly before firing—"I'm not really all *that* capable." *Bang!*

In order to create, we must open. In opening, we experience the tingling of awakened energy that signals the flow of creative juices. As our senses become more acute, the unfamiliar sensation of energetic expansion may have a disquieting effect: *Do I have to keep this up forever? It feels like I'm going too fast. I might fly apart, or even, go crazy.*

What if some part of me escapes and does damage to myself or others? Irrational as these fears sound, it is not unusual to experience feelings of losing control, being devoured, or being overwhelmed when standing on the threshold of new possibilities.

As the force of inspiration moves us to do things we have never done before, we may experience an unsettling realization—we don't really know who we are anymore. Dislocation and disorientation frequently accompany creative transformation: *Who am I? Is this a new beginning? Or the beginning of the end?* When we can't be certain where the strength of desire will take us, resistance arrives like a knight in shining armor to rescue us from the threat of losing control and perhaps ourselves in the process. Like Sheri, we have spent so many years backing away from our own potential, that when we start to open up to it—*when we actually start to succeed*—it can feel unsafe. As Marianne Williamson writes, "It is our light, not our darkness, that most frightens us."

········●

We cherish momentum; we hate going backwards or feeling stuck. Regardless, we need to accept the fact that resistance begins the gradual process of trusting and freeing our desire. We stretch a little and then pull back a lot, stretch a little farther and retreat a little less, two steps forward one back, five steps forward six back, three steps forward half a step back . . . and so it goes until little by little we find that our capacities have grown to meet the challenge.

What you do after hitting the wall determines the course of your path. The strength of your aversion means that something just beneath the surface wants to emerge. Resistance signals you to get ready. Stop struggling. Breathe. A breakthrough looms just around the corner.

The wisest creators respond to reluctance with the simple question,

What is needed? Then they listen intently for a response from within. Retreating may provide a peaceful and necessary respite. At other times, we need to toughen up, dig deeper, and persevere. Often, the best strategy may be to relax, do something else for a while, and wait. When that doesn't work, we may need to try another way around, discovering something new and unexpected.

By exploring resistance, we ultimately re-energize our creative vitality. Creative energy moves in cycles; it cannot always flow. We alternately close down and reach out, contract and expand, over and over again. Each time we emerge from a period of resistance, we come to a deeper understanding of how we ourselves inhabit creative mystery.

Further Reflections On Resistance

By turns cunning, baffling, and mysterious, resistance can be difficult to track. Cultivate self-awareness to see where your thoughts and feelings are taking you. If you wish to go deeper, explore one or more of the following questions. *Write, draw, dance, paint, meditate . . .*

➥ Where am I stuck? Which specific tasks, feelings, or thoughts associated with the creative process do I dislike? Why?

➥ What challenges in my work or personal life am I avoiding? What thoughts, feelings or memories arise when I attempt to engage those challenges?

➥ What precisely is my method for NOT DOING what I think I want to do? Does my resistance show up as impatience, ambivalence, poor work habits, inflexibility, self-doubt, chronic anxiety, or as something else?

☞ Do I feel free to make up my own mind, to set my own course, or do I feel pressured? What is the source of the pressure? How might I address it?

☞ To help me negotiate with negativity, how might I develop the following positive qualities: awareness, attention, kindness, willingness, curiosity, commitment, optimism, and delight?

☞ What helps me remember the dream, the need, the love, the sheer fun that inspired me to begin this journey?

☞ What patterns, relationships, or things do I cling to that may be holding me back? Am I willing to let go? Am I willing to change?

☞ Where do I sabotage myself because I am afraid that I can't have what I want? What keeps me from dreaming bigger?

☞ Which is worse: the *short-term discomfort* of actually doing what I need to do or the *long-term guilt* I feel when I don't?

☞ What activities or practices might facilitate the transition from resistance to action?

*The ability to suffer and even appreciate pain is no
less basic to creative vision than the joy of discovery.*

—Robert Grudin

*The process of making art is a process of confronting
oneself, one's lack of talent, one's lack of confidence.*

—Rod MacIver

*Only through experience of trial and suffering
can the soul be strengthened, ambition inspired,
and success achieved.*

—Helen Keller

Suffering

IT'S EASY TO HAVE INTERESTS and hobbies that don't challenge you at a
deep level. But whatever you give your heart to is bound to be really,
really tough. Creators who care deeply—particularly when the process
becomes difficult—will organize their lives around their creative work,
even though their lives could be a lot easier and a lot more fun if they
weren't pursuing their passion.

When I began my journey to recover creative confidence, I had no
idea that suffering would be part of the deal. I only knew I was lonely
and lost and that something was drawing me deeper beneath the surface. Like many seekers, I hungered for a way to live a more connected
life. I thought the creative process would be my salvation. Being young
and idealistic, I worshipped the god of self-expression. I thought that
if I could discover my talents and apply them to some noble purpose,

I would save myself. I believed that by living the right kind of life my suffering would end.

So much for youthful hopes.

It has taken a lot of hard growing for me to stop fighting with creative pain—to accept the kind of *necessary suffering* that comes with intense personal expression. I never feel as alone and full of doubt as I do when I am writing. I have also never been so engaged, fulfilled, or connected.

When we focus deeply, when we give so much of ourselves to something that matters, it becomes both a joy and a burden. The paradox of the creative process is this: Intense personal expression makes us feel vulnerable because it comes from the deepest part of us, but dropping down into those fathomless depths nourishes the creator's soul.

Suffering frequently feels more like failure than a gateway to growth. Yet when experienced with awareness and acceptance, suffering can grant a measure of wisdom that functions as a source of inspiration as well as a comforting bedrock of inner confidence.

But . . .

there is creative pain and then there is the pain we create.

·····゠·‥●

Carl Jung, the Swiss psychiatrist and psychological theorist, said it best: "Neurosis is always a substitute for legitimate suffering." In attempting to unravel the quagmire of emotional pain, we need to distinguish between two important categories of suffering: unnecessary and necessary.

Unnecessary suffering results from our resistance to doing what is required to fulfill our dreams. It stems almost entirely from our hidden agendas and repeated patterns of self-sabotage. This pain could be avoided but for our faulty reasoning, inconsistent work habits, lifestyle choices, and lack of self-awareness that leave us too distracted or depleted for creative work. Whatever genuine adversities may have befallen us, we bring ourselves much needless additional suffering by perpetuating those injuries through vacillation and misguided impulse.

Necessary suffering is something else.
It cannot be avoided.
It's the price we pay to grow creatively.

Becoming proficient at your craft takes work and sacrifice, often for years. Aspiring creators sometimes like to bask in the reflected light of successful creators. We watch from the sidelines, perhaps secretly envying their fame—not to mention their fortune. But for every one of those luminaries who flashes an effortless smile, there are thousands of talented creators toiling anonymously to master their craft.

The process of mastery involves *necessary* suffering. The anxiety of our efforts, the many setbacks and reversals—even the daily frustrations of simply learning how to do something—can feel humiliating, especially for those of us with fragile egos. Much of the creative process seems to involve a painful confrontation with our sense of personal inadequacy, whether in the form of fear, guilt, loneliness, doubt, or even abject self-loathing. Depending on our personal history, sensitivities, and temperament, many of us simply cannot bear that kind of shame.

·····⋅⋅•

The powerful and particularly acute form of suffering known as *shame* plays a complex role in the creative process. Everyone feels shame at one time or another. A healthy sense of shame keeps a creator's outsized ego in check. It also helps us realize when our self-absorption becomes hurtful to the people we love. Suffering a certain amount of shame may even nurture creative ambition.

As an impressionable child, I felt deeply ashamed watching my mother's chronic helplessness. Her inability to be a force in her own life, to direct even a modicum of her considerable talents was more than a disappointment—it was a shameful failure. Despite the considerable anguish I suffered at the time, the embarrassment I internalized at such a young age fueled my determination to work through my own impediments. For creators who seek redemption from a previous disgrace, shame can be a powerful engine that drives them forward into the rebirth found through the act of creation.

More often than not, however, shame becomes a barrier to accomplishment. Where guilt says, "I *did* something wrong," shame says: "I *am* something wrong." Toxic levels of suffering caused by such a shame-based identity corrode a creator's sense of power and agency. Shame floods the body with a piercing sense of unworthiness. In these moments, our suffering compels us to retreat from whatever is associated with this intolerable feeling—even from our own gifts and talents. The natural impulse to express becomes extinguished by unendurable self-consciousness. Over time, it becomes difficult, if not impossible, to risk the unmoored explorations and naked self-exposure required of creators.

When the grip of shame paralyzes us, telling ourselves to stay positive may not be enough. Sometimes, we need to heal. *Healing* begins once we confront the *unnecessary* suffering caused by relentless self-rejection. During the healing process, we come to terms with who we are and the life experiences that have had a hand in shaping us. We move from being victims to beneficiaries of our past. Healing grants the great grace of acceptance.

But I always thought I needed to change myself in order to heal? The essence of a person never really changes. During the healing process, what ends up changing is your relationship with yourself, especially the parts of yourself you try to hide. But *that* change changes everything else. Self-acceptance allows deeper access to your innate rhythms. As self-trust grows, you willingly embrace those aspects of life you used to avoid or struggle to control. In coming more fully alive, you still suffer of course, because creativity never comes easily. As one of my clients remarked, "I no longer take the discomforts of the process so personally, and that makes the struggles with my work more manageable. I'm finally getting somewhere!"

······ ·· ●

The creative process thrives in a condition of wholeness. Creators balance the necessity of being alert and receptive to the nuance of feeling with the equally important necessity for bold and decisive action. To achieve this balance, our inner lives need to be lived, not fixed— explored, not ignored. But our extroverted, can-do culture wants to fix everything; if it can't be fixed, then we throw it away.

Conditioned by the Western cultural model, we have learned a harmful habit of throwing away the parts of ourselves that we deem deficient or defective. In doing so, we make outcasts of these throw-away selves. Cast adrift, they resent us and seek to undermine us, their oppressors and detractors. *Unnecessary* suffering springs from this internal battle for dominance and survival. Like wars in the outer world, waging a war within can be costly in terms of energy and resources that could be better spent. Over time, this cycle of shaming and retaliation cannibalizes our creative assets.

As creators, we venture into the hidden corners of consciousness. While most people feel no need to investigate the forgotten regions of the mind, blocked creators who want to break free rarely have a choice in the matter. The unhealed wounds surrounding our suffering can hold creative energy hostage for decades or even forever. Ask yourself: *How badly do I want to reach my creative potential? Badly enough to endure the necessary pain of healing my wounds?*

·····˙··●

One of the truly crippling sufferings in life is the inability to share our gifts. While our creative energies remain trapped, we inhabit an airless, lifeless desert. Whatever we withhold metamorphoses into a heavy burden and eventually can make us sick. As the flow of creative energy stagnates, it becomes a breeding ground for illness and unremitting unhappiness.

Most people reach the end of their days wishing they had taken more chances in their lives, not fewer. We tend to regret the things we didn't do rather than the things we did. As a child bearing witness to my mother's tragic self-destruction, I learned a life-defining lesson. Decades later, I found that lesson confirmed in the Gnostic Gospel of Thomas: "If you bring forth what is within you, what you bring forth will save you; if you do not bring forth what is within you, what you do not bring forth will destroy you."

No matter the source of your suffering, you can always heal. You only have to *be willing* to encounter the *necessary* suffering inherent in the healing process—just like in the creative process itself. Healing may begin as a dawning recognition in the privacy of your own mind. Only later does the journey deepen in its intensity, becoming more focused, perhaps in the company of a trusted teacher, mentor, or therapist.

The seventeenth-century poet and theologian François Fénelon understood that wisdom can arise from *necessary* suffering. When we expose the shame that binds our creative energies, our faults become fully and excruciatingly magnified by the light of awareness. That's when "a whole swarm of shameful feelings, like filthy reptiles, crawl out from a hidden cave. We could never have believed that we harbored such things and we stand aghast as we watch them gradually appear." Although we may find it difficult to tolerate the realization of shame, let alone stay in our bodies long enough to heal, this needn't be a cause for worry or despair. On the contrary, when we finally, as Fénelon states, "perceive our malady" (aka "come out of denial"), our restoration has already commenced.

We often prove stronger than we imagined. By integrating, rather than rejecting, the unwanted and painful aspects of ourselves and our experience, we calm fearful resistance while developing the requisite depth and maturity to take our creativity to new levels. Once we experience the value of *necessary* suffering, we can engage it with confidence, welcoming it as a working partner in the creative process.

Further Reflections On Suffering

Consider the wisdom of French author Marcel Proust: "We are only healed of a suffering by experiencing it to the full." If you wish to go deeper, explore one or more of the following questions. *Write, draw, dance, paint, meditate . . .*

☞ Am I more concerned with alleviating pain, or with understanding its message? What may be struggling to reveal itself to me through my pain? What remains unhealed in my heart?

☞ What unspoken issues are causing me to feel perpetually dissatisfied, unable to engage? How do my patterns of thinking, feeling, and behaving contribute to my suffering? I'd like to move forward— which specific patterns currently undermine my progress?

➥ What parts of myself have I banished? If I must reconnect with the soft, tender places to break the impasse, am I willing to be *that* vulnerable for the sake of achieving my heart's desire?

➥ Where in my body do I experience these feelings: anger, shame, fear, grief, self-doubt, despair, resentment? What memories arise?

➥ How does the way I engage or disconnect from my negative feelings impact my creativity? What are my ideas for channeling the power of emotional energy into creative expression?

➥ Whose voices do I hear in my head? Which ones do I listen to?

➥ When I make a mistake or receive critical feedback, do I consider it part of the process or feel it as a fatal flaw?

➥ How have I been able to persevere through *necessary* suffering in the past? What crucial lessons and unexpected benefits emerged?

➥ How has *unnecessary* suffering begun to overwhelm my ability to focus on my creative work? Is it time to consider getting help from a professional?

➥ Consider Viktor Frankel: "What is to give light must endure burning."

*Perhaps everything terrible is in its deepest being
something helpless that wants help from us.*

—Rainer Maria Rilke

*We are simply asked to shift focus and to take on
more gentle perception. Just one sincere surrendered
moment, when love matters more than anything.*

—Marianne Williamson

*Speak quietly to yourself and promise there will
be better days.*

—Mary Anne Radmacher

Compassion

WHEN WHATEVER WE TRY FAILS, when we reach our wit's end, when we
want to tear out our hair because that seems better than sticking with
the project, we need to step back and treat ourselves with compassion.
Many creators too frequently blame themselves for their fears and
frustrations. *How could I be so stupid? What's wrong with me? Why didn't I
know that? I'll never be able to make this work. Why do I even bother to try?*
I hear these sorts of uncharitable responses from clients all the time.
And I am, of course, guilty of them myself. When something goes
wrong, I find it far too easy to blame myself.

Reacting from fear and anger is human—but usually not helpful.
Liberating creative energy depends on how compassionately we respect
the sensibilities of our inner child. It's a package deal—along with
insatiable curiosity and unbridled enthusiasm comes tenderness and

vulnerability. Juggling adult responsibilities keeps us preoccupied and distanced from the emotional delicacies of childhood. This makes it difficult to recognize the many ways we may be reinjuring ourselves emotionally as we go about the practical business of being productive.

No matter your current chronological age, your inner child is never too far away. Close your eyes for a moment. Take a breath. As you slowly exhale, recall a moment from the past when you found yourself in a troubling predicament: How do the people closest to you respond? Perhaps it is a parent, a friend, a teacher, or other authority figure. Picture the scene in your mind's eye. Listen to the tone of voice. Do they focus on the problem at hand, or on you? Do they offer their help and support in figuring out an alternative course of action? Do they let you know that you remain worthwhile even if they are displeased with your behavior? Or are they sarcastic, demeaning, or disparaging? Do they speak harshly and then abruptly break off the connection by walking out? Or is some other punishment forthcoming?

The loneliness and shame of feeling like a bad person can be one of the most devastating consequences of getting into trouble. When we are in trouble creatively, when we are not working well, when the world has disappointed us, the last thing we need is to inflict more emotional suffering by scolding ourselves. Ask yourself: *What did I learn from my early experiences about how I should treat myself when I am in trouble?*

······⋅··●

In one of those weird cases of life imitating art, ever since I started writing this chapter I have been increasingly uninspired and adrift. Today, I realize that I am feeling overwhelmed by the colossal challenge of the task still before me. For the moment, at least, it feels like I'm drifting off course.

I've lost the point of it all.
(Did I have one to begin with?)
I am *having* trouble. I am *in* trouble.
(Sometimes, it's hard to tell the difference.)

Without a sense of direction I could be going in circles and not even know it. In a blizzard you can be a block from home or twenty miles away, but you can't tell because all you can see are vast stretches of whiteness. Or, maybe it's more like an ocean crossing. When I was sailing in the Caribbean, I remember vividly the scary feeling of losing sight of the shore and the security of familiar landmarks. Right now, it feels as if I am treading water in the middle of a lonely ocean: There's nothing but empty horizon for miles and miles, no bit of land, no tiny island, nothing but my own confused and disheartened mind for company.

So naturally, the marketing director at the publishing company calls this afternoon. When she asks me how I'm doing, I stupidly think she really wants to know. So I confess my lack of focus, hoping to hear some cheery words of support like, "Oh, don't worry about it, let's have a meeting." I mean, what do I know? I just figure business people have meetings to solve problems.

Instead, she tells me SHE'S having trouble: "There are so many books out there on creativity, the market is just glutted with them. I've got to have a *handle* in order to sell *Wild Ideas* and I can't find one."

A handle??? *Immediately, my mind pictures a tidy handbag, a smart leather model with sturdy reinforced handles, the kind I imagine well-coiffed women in Beverly Hills carry. Gucci, perhaps.*

She asks me to describe the book's "promise" in twenty-five words or less. Instinctively, I understand that I must come up with something brilliant, but I can't manage even a breath of enthusiasm, let alone a coherent sentence. I'm completely tongue-tied and mumble something about having a bad day. "I'll have to call you back," I finally manage to reply.

Am I *in* trouble? Or *having* trouble?

(It's hard to tell the difference.)

It is a fateful moment. One of those moments in which you think that everything in the universe—or at least everything in *your* universe—seems to depend on a single conversation. Instead, an unbridgeable chasm opens between two people. I know I have just blown it. Badly. Without actually saying it, the marketing director wanted me to give her a reason to stand by me and I couldn't. I didn't know what to say to convince her I was worthy.

Bending over my desk, I cradle my head in my arms, letting the sourness of the day weigh on me. How am I supposed to help her believe in this project when I can't even believe in it myself? THE WALL between me and my creative spark doesn't get much bigger than this. And, right now, I surely don't have the energy to scale it.

I'm *having* trouble. I'm *in* trouble.

(It's hard to tell the difference.)

Cut off from my internal sources of inspiration and comfort, I feel creatively destitute. Instead of encouraging myself to sit down and tackle that twenty-five words or less pitch, I feel utterly trapped by my inexperience. I expend valuable emotional energy spinning crippling fantasies of humiliation as I see myself attempting to explain the embarrassing turn of events: . . . *Well, uh, you see it's like this, it's a business and, well . . . I just don't have what it takes.* Bang!

I am definitely *in* trouble.

When the marketing director calls back the next morning, I am standing in my bathrobe holding a cup of tea in both hands. Her saccharine tone belies her murderous intentions: "You know Cathy, I just love this book. *I love everything about Wild Ideas.* The problem is, no one knows who you are—you are a nameless commodity. I am sure you are aware that not many unknown writers succeed on their first attempt. It just isn't fair to you for us to publish it and then not be able to sell it."

I have nothing to offer.

Double Bang!

I am in Hell.

·······•

As creators, we all eventually enter our own private version of creative hell. At such desperate times, the challenge of finding a compassionate response is never more urgent. Regardless of how we got here, our power lies in recognizing that we always have a choice about how to respond.

Compassion brings a loving response to injury.

When I hang up the phone, I can feel my panic rising. I take a quick intake of breath and begin an all too familiar litany of self-blame when suddenly I stop. There is already enough damage, I don't need to inflict any more on myself. The situation calls for tenderness.

Compassion looks at our human reactivity and then chooses a response from a deeper level.

Sometimes you have to take your own hand, as though you were a lost child. I sit down and begin writing a letter to comfort myself. (If you are struggling to find your way, I hope these words will comfort you too.)

"I understand that you feel hopeless right now. You're at the half-way point and that's always a difficult time in the life of a project. You can't go back and you can't see the end. It feels like being adrift in a dark and endless sea. It's natural to be afraid you might never reach your destination. But this stage will pass. I believe you have something worthwhile here, so let's keep going. I know it can be difficult to accept, not everyone will grasp your vision—but that doesn't mean you won't eventually find an audience. The important thing now is not to give up. You will figure something out when the time comes."

("But what if we caaan't?" whines a tiny voice from the dark.)

"Come on now, you haven't even tried yet. The Universe sent us this amazing opportunity that didn't work out the way we had hoped. But, we have an exciting concept, a good start, and a partially completed project to finish. This disappointment isn't the end. It's the beginning of a new chapter!"

This is vital: *You really do need to make the effort to encourage yourself when things are not going well—just like you would if you were consoling a friend.* Even if it does not come naturally, with practice, you can learn to be kinder to yourself. You can learn to break the vicious cycle of self-criticism and blaming. In so doing, you will encourage the very best in yourself, nurturing reserves of resilience that will repay your efforts tenfold.

······˙··●

We become incredibly anxious about how we feel, but, in many instances, we don't really need an immediate solution. All we really need is a willingness to engage with a tender, empathetic heart. Once we develop the confidence to respond to our feelings, we cease to fear the vicissitudes of the creative journey and we can open to whatever comes our way.

One final caveat: Never confuse compassion with indulgence. *A soft heart is not weak.* Compassion acknowledges responsibility and seeks to make amends where necessary. We need to honor our commitments and relationships—which is to say, we need to be ruthlessly honest with ourselves. When we mess up, compassion comforts, while gently turning us toward the path of truth.

During my encounter with the marketing director, I felt unfairly blindsided. But I had also been terribly naive, inexperienced, and too trusting. Based on our earlier conversations, I had thought the company would take care of me. I grossly underestimated how sweeping economic pressures, just beginning to impact the publishing industry at the time, were quickly changing the culture and priorities of this small idealistic publishing company. During the year we worked together, the company's mission morphed from "nurturing and developing new writers" to one in which their survival depended on acclamation and the certainty of blockbuster profits.

It was a difficult lesson, but I learned never to take anything for granted. I learned what now seems obvious: I can't put myself and the future of my creative work in someone else's hands. I can't simply be *the artist*; I also need to be a savvy businesswoman. I promised myself: The next time I am in that position, I will be ready.

In the creative process, love is our ally and partner. Practicing self-compassion makes it safer to take life-changing chances, make embarrassing mistakes, suffer the consequences, grow from painful lessons and losses—and nurture the confidence to try again.

Further Reflections On Compassion

Compassion recognizes the need to face pain in order to learn and evolve. If you wish to go deeper, explore one or more of the following questions. *Write, draw, dance, paint, meditate . . .*

☞ What are the practical and tangible ways that I care for my myself when I'm feeling discouraged or disappointed? What brings me back to my passion?

☞ In what ways am I too hard on myself? What am I still holding against myself? How often do I compare my path with others' and find myself coming up short?

☞ What negative thoughts do I have about myself? When do they tend to surface during the creative process? How do I deal with them?

☞ When things aren't going well, do I obsess about my inadequacies or encourage myself to keep going? Am I able to remind myself that there are a lot of other people who share my feelings or do I feel separated from others?

☞ If someone has hurt or disappointed me, do I wonder what might be going on from their point of view or do I take their behavior personally?

☞ Do I have a palpable connection with my inner child? What situations bring this aspect of my early identity to the surface? What are the child's helpful and disruptive effects on my creativity? If my inner child could speak, what would he or she say to me?

*Sometimes courage is the quiet voice at the end of the
day saying, 'I will try again tomorrow.'*

—Mary Anne Radmacher

*There are always difficulties arising that tempt you
to believe your critics are right. To take a course of
action and follow it to the end requires courage.*

—Ralph Waldo Emerson

*Such courage it takes to believe in ourselves . . .
Such pain to get to where we want to be.*

—Connie Fowler

Courage

ALTHOUGH THERE WERE MANY TIMES during this project when I felt like
quitting, I was especially vulnerable after the relationship with my
publisher ended. With so much at stake, our breakup confirmed my
worst fears: If I trust someone, I will be abandoned.

> *And then . . . I fell into a chasm of shame.*
> *Oh, the pain. The pain.*

Rejection had cracked open the wounds of the past. There would be
no getting around this one, no way to distract myself, and no way to
will myself to go on, either. I had to take the hit. I would decide later
if there was a compelling enough reason to keep going now that the
worst had happened.

The worst had happened.
Oh, the pain.

I spend a few days in the fetal position, feeling the kind of pain that starts in your stomach and radiates out through your entire body—even my fingers ache. Everything that has ever hurt me washes through. I tumble into a black hole: There is no up or down, only tumult and noxious fumes. I feel sick with doubt, and have vowed never to write another word—so long as I live. It seems hard to believe that just a few short weeks ago, I was riding a wave of confidence and support that promised to carry me safely to shore: "Everyone is so happy with the pages you sent," gushed my editor.

Like a baby taking its first steps, I had felt myself picking up momentum. Now, I have been knocked flat on my ass.

One morning, I decide I will try to get out of bed. When I attempt to extend my limbs, a stabbing sensation rises up from my belly, so not moving seems like the best solution. Somewhere in the back of my mind I hear a distant shout: "This isn't personal!" Someone inside me tries to throw a lifeline, but it seems like too much work to reach for it. I have the momentum of inertia going for me now. Besides, I'm not ready to throw off this comforting blanket of defeat.

Not yet.

Days pass and the distance from that crushing phone call grows ever longer. One day, I receive several inquiries from people eagerly anticipating this book, and, somehow, I hang onto that interest like a drowning woman clutching a life preserver. The world stops swirling and I start answering the phone again . . . and,

Now what?

······˙··●

We tend to think of courage as gallant action in the face of imminent death. Movies starring John Wayne, Bruce Willis, or Angelina Jolie come to mind. And that is one type of courage. *Heroic courage* speaks to the larger-than-life ideal of steeling yourself against your feelings and charging forward, seemingly untouched by whatever's happening around you. Unquestionably, we need a certain toughness to navigate the creative process, particularly when we must convince others of our project's merit in the face of extreme skepticism or outright rejection.

My experience of working with many brave people teaches me that often courage must be wrestled out from under something massive and heavy and dark. The bravest people do not feel brave; they more often feel riddled with doubt and inadequacy. As the psychologist Rollo May once wrote, "Courage is not the absence of despair; it is, rather, the capacity to move ahead in spite of despair." Doubt—about our direction, about our abilities, about the value of our work—becomes integral to the process of discovering the depth of our courage.

······˙··●

When the bottom falls out, when we can't find anything to grasp, we face a crisis of confidence that raises the question of whether or not to continue the journey: *Is it worth it?* The decision to move ahead despite a big setback requires tremendous bravery because we have to change our way of perceiving the situation in order to regroup.

Wild Ideas began as a collaboration with a publisher. I never would have taken on such an extensive project on my own. There was enormous ego gratification in being chosen over other, more experienced writers. I felt flattered, desirable, wanted. Caught up in the excitement of a new opportunity, I gave away my power without even realizing it. Inadvertently, I staked the future of my book on a flimsy foundation—my motivation to create became tied to the support and approval of others. Now, that support had been withdrawn and I was paying the price: My self-esteem hit a new low.

I have a big job ahead of me.

Recovering personal power and rekindling inspiration in the face of loss (whether it takes the form of disappointment, failure, or rejection), calls upon self-knowledge and inner strength. The word "courage" derives from the French word *coeur*, meaning "heart." Perhaps what we really need in order to persist is *heart-strength*.

I try to recall other periods in my life when circumstances seemed similarly dark and insurmountable—times when I felt betrayed by a broken promise or disappointed in myself. How did I make it through? What resources did I call on from within myself?

I remember that courage has many faces and frequently appears in conjunction with other feelings. Courage can seem like *anger*. There's nothing like someone telling me that I CAN'T do something to ignite a furious passion: "Oh, yeah, just watch me." When I feel challenged by adversity, I am more likely to find the strength to carry on.

Sometimes, courage bears a close resemblance to *love*. From the beginning, the heartfelt desire to share what I have learned has inspired me to do what seemed beyond my capacities. That desire still smolders, buried temporarily under the ashes of doubt.

At other times, courage appears in the guise of *patience*. Waiting, exploring, staying with the pain—struggling to find the meaning in it—instead of giving up and turning away.

Finally, courage emerges as *faith*. Engaging the creative process means learning to grow from the unexpected. Perhaps the most difficult kind of courage is simply trusting the journey itself. Continuing

the journey, especially after heartbreaking disappointment, can sometimes be the ultimate act of courage.

·····.·..●

It is one thing to have big courage—the sort of bold strength that is
needed to overcome unforeseen challenges—but it is quite another to
have the small sort of unglamorous courage for the daily persistence
required for creative work. Within the day-to-day process of creating,
every new encounter with our work requires a separate act of courage.
We constantly begin. It doesn't matter if we are three-quarters through
a first draft of a novel, a musical score, or a painting. Each time we go
into our offices and studios, we must find the strength to begin again.
Such inward courage is called *character*.

Much of this routine courage helps a creator cope with the constant
uncertainty of outcome while juggling the conflicting demands of the
process itself. A creative mind must balance ever-present dualities:
abandon and restraint, spontaneity and planning, willpower and willingness, fear and trust, doubt and confidence, laziness and ambition,
despair and hope, feeling and thinking, solitude and community,
personal integrity and the demands of the marketplace. Like a high-wire
performer, this kind of quiet courage walks a mental and emotional
tightrope that eventually becomes a way of life.

·····.·..●

Bear in mind that not every project merits the tremendous effort
needed for completion, and some visions can't be translated into reality.
Foolish courage persists in ignoring your limits or trying to do or be
something you are not. Letting go frees you to move on. The attempt
may have failed—but YOU are not a failure. The act of giving up

recognizes that a particular project has no juice left or that the timing isn't right—it does not end your creative life.

One day in the spring, I wake up feeling better. I am slowly coming back to myself. I walk, I read, I eat, I sleep, I garden, I make love. I continue to write. I am not trying to accomplish anything in particular. It comforts me to keep working at what I have started. I will find my way simply by making the decision to say no to fear and yes to the vision of myself as a published author. If somewhere along the way, I discover that my manuscript is seriously flawed and beyond resuscitation—if that time should come—I hope I will have the grace to surrender, the compassion not to berate myself, and the wisdom to recognize other options.

But that day is not today.

······ ··●

Whatever your situation, life presents you with continuous opportunities for working with anxiety. Creative courage grows with every experience in which you face down fear in order to do the thing you believe you cannot do. At times, the necessity of what you feel compelled to do is apparent only to yourself. And still you must act. The sort of lonely assertion of self that precedes any creative act echoes a series of quiet choices that ultimately define your character, while moving you, sometimes imperceptibly, toward completion.

Ultimately, courage supports that which we value. If we value our dreams, we will delve deeply into ourselves to discover the fortitude to give them wings.

Further Reflections On Courage

You don't need to feel confident to have courage. You gain courage and confidence each time you stop and face your fears. If you wish to go deeper, explore one or more of the following questions. *Write, draw, dance, paint, meditate . . .*

☞ In what areas of my life do I have difficulty finding courage?

☞ In what ways do I hold myself back because the opinions or actions of others cause me to doubt myself? What would I do differently if I felt sufficient courage?

☞ In what situations do I cast blame instead of taking responsibility? What payoffs have I gotten from thinking like a victim?

☞ What do I tell myself when I encounter criticism? How can I learn to find the truth in criticism so I can grow?

☞ Where has fear caused me to give up too quickly? What current projects or circumstances require greater perseverance?

☞ Do I have the courage to change my mind, or do I hold fast to my point of view because I need to be right?

☞ What failures have made me stronger? Can I think of a time when I suffered a setback that seemed insurmountable, yet kept going? What did that situation show me about where my courage lies?

☞ When I consider taking action on something scary, what is the worst that could happen? (Failure? Rejection? Embarrassment? Disappointment? Loss?) Are my fears warning me about a realistic possibility for which I can actually prepare, or am I more afraid of the unknown and the possibility of losing control? If the worst happens am I resilient enough to recover? What are the possible rewards and benefits of taking this action?

☞ What helps me find the inner strength to keep going? What kind of support will help me cultivate courage?

☞ Consider this: When you feel you want to give up and you can't go much further, look at how far you have come. The courage that has brought you this far will be the strength that carries you the rest of the way.

It always comes down to the same necessity; go deep enough and there is a bedrock of truth, however hard.

—*May Sarton*

There are times when we stop. We sit still. We lose
ourselves in a pile of leaves or its memory. We listen
and breezes from a whole other world begin to whisper.
Then we begin our "going down."

—James Carroll

. . . we're meant to go down deeply into our own wells
so that we finally reach the stream that's the source.

—Ira Progoff

You have to be able to recognize your own depths.

—Joseph Campbell

4
Going
Deep

FEW SIGNIFICANT CHALLENGES can be solved by relying on intellect alone. Sooner or later, after all the wondering, exploring, researching, and hard thinking, you will reach the limits of the conscious mind. When you don't know where to go, when you can't move forward, go deeper. It's time to stop wrestling, and turn it all over to the unconscious mind.

Working incessantly on a problem can be counterproductive. Frequently the harder we try, the more elusive the solution. Creative frustration often means that a problem cannot be resolved at the same level of thinking that created it. Relaxing conscious attention encourages a creative partnership between the rational mind and the intuitive mind. At this stage, creators release the self-conscious effort of thinking and doing. While the analytical mind rests, deeper insight ripens.

Letting go is not the same as giving up. Putting the question, problem, or project aside for a while opens a space for answers—but only if we can sustain the opening. A period of emptying and receptivity generally precedes revelation.

All this lack of structure sounds scary to me. I don't like feeling out of control. It can be difficult to trust in something you can't yet see or touch. Even though nothing of outward significance appears to be occurring, something deep inside you busily works on the problem— it's just that the activity takes place at such a wordless level you scarcely know anything is happening. With practice you will learn to count on the *deeper mind* and work with it as an important ally.

In a creative life, we need to be creating *ourselves* along with our work. Most of the time, we skim along the surface, barely stopping long enough to take a breath. One of the ways we can move our work forward is by living more deeply. The process of deepening is a journey into a different aspect of existence—one that lies beyond our busy, workaday reality. Like mythical heroes, we leave the solid, visible world in order to descend into the mysterious realms of hidden knowledge. We enter a silent sea, becoming receptive to deeper and more ancient rhythms. When we cross the boundary of conscious knowledge, we dive deep into a kind of direct inner knowing that inspires new directions and solutions far more profound and elegant than anything we could have deduced through reasoning alone. Ask yourself: *What unexpected resources might I discover if I dive even deeper?*

Qualities that support incubation of the problem and communion with the deep self include *mystery, mourning, patience, trust,* and *intuition.*

Mystery shelters and gestates seeds of insight in the depths of our unconscious. *Mourning* releases outmoded ideas, expectations, and behavior, making room for a new range of possibilities. *Patience* waits while ideas ripen outside of our control. *Trust* believes that something is happening even when we can't see it. *Intuition* contacts deep knowledge, which triggers breakthrough (Aha!) and reentry into the conscious world.

The unknown is seen differently, as mystery,
something to move toward, not something to avoid,
something which increases one's sense of wonder,
one's sense of aliveness.

—Rachel Naomi Remen

The answer is never the answer. What's really
interesting is the mystery.

—Ken Kesey

The mystery of life is not a problem to be solved but a
reality to be experienced.

—Aart van der Leeuw

Mystery

MUCH OF THE UNIVERSE lies outside our understanding. The more we open to our creativity, the more we realize how little we know. Often, our need to try to explain everything, our drive to answer every why and how with a carefully measured and reasoned reply, inhibits the sense of wonder and delight needed to fuel creation. Answers matter, but people cannot live joyfully without, as Einstein put it, "standing rapt in awe" at the amazing spectacle and beauty of creation.

I recall a coastal outing with my father when I was in my early thirties. We are walking along a trail to the marsh when suddenly a slow-moving shadow darkens the blue above. My father and I gaze up to witness a precision formation of birds furiously flapping their wings —hundreds of black wings beating against a cloudless blue expanse. A holy silence descends over our small patch of earth as everything recedes into the magnificence of sky and bird and primordial quiet. This rare moment of sudden penetration—so charged with the transcendent power of beauty—connects me to something larger than myself.

When normal time resumes, I turn to my father in breathless wonderment, hoping to share the ecstatic moment. He beams a broad smile but once he begins to speak, I realize that his experience has been quite different from my own. In response to my "Wow, wasn't that amazing!" he excitedly begins speculating on the species of bird, where they came from, and where they are going.

"But Dad . . ." I stop myself mid-sentence and recognize my unanswered longing. I want to savor and share nature's awe-inspiring spectacle—I couldn't care less about naming it.

So there we stood, my father and I: two witnesses to the same event, each with a different story. The physician and the artist. The gap between us was as familiar to me as the breadth of sky that encompassed us both. While my father sought further clarification of fact and reason, to anchor the unexpected in time and place, I was focused on my feelings. I wanted to be taken and transformed by my experience; I had no wish to tame it. On the contrary, I wanted to be swept up in the intoxicating power of nature's majesty, to let it overwhelm me and stir within me something unpredictable. I preferred to let the birds—along with their origins and destination—remain a mystery.

The creative process asks us to bridge that same gap. Within each of us there exists a similar dichotomy between the rational part of us that looks for answers, that strives to explain the unexplainable, and the part of us that seeks the pleasure and intensity of pure sensation as a gateway to intuitive and sacred knowledge.

Logical inquiry, and the intellectual bounty it yields, contributes valuable knowledge about our world. But it often does so at a cost of distancing us from our subjective experience and stripping away the miraculous. Not all mysteries require solutions: "The eye goes blind when it *only* wants to see why" (my italics), wrote the mystical poet Rumi.

Our capacity to be continually surprised by life's mysteries nourishes the creative spirit. When we allow some mysteries to remain intact, they open the heart, uplift the spirit, and connect us to something beyond the visible world. The most gifted creators order the chaos of experience without sacrificing the freshness and luminosity of the mystery that inspired the work.

······`··●

Creativity unfolds from hidden places of mystery and incompletion that reside within the human heart; these places hunger for connection and self-expression. Sometimes surrender may be the best strategy for recovering an unanswered longing. Surrendering to our own internal mystery empowers us in ways we cannot predict. In the enigmatic landscape of our interior being, we find more than empty expanses that threaten to engulf us; we also find the fertile beauty that inspires poets, theologians, and philosophers.

At her first appointment, Sara assures me that she is "the most uncreative person in the whole world." I make an attempt to reframe the situation. "Would it be all right if we proceed with a different assumption for the rest of the session? Let's pretend that you *are* creative, but you just misplaced that part of yourself and forgot where you put it." Sara purses her lips in doubt but seems willing to go along. I ask Sara to close her eyes. "Without thinking, quickly place your hand on the spot in your body where your creativity might be hiding." Sara immediately covers her lower abdomen with her hands, as if protecting herself. I encourage Sara to go a little further. "With your mind's eye, look into that place under your hands and tell me what you see or sense."

"There's nothing but black space," she quickly retorts—"I *already* told you, there's nothing in there!" Seeking relief from her agitation, Sara opens her eyes. I gently invite her to return to the blackness so that we can explore it together. "I, uh . . . I know this sounds crazy," she begins hesitantly, "but it feels like I might fall in there. What if I can't come out again?"

Sara's face begins to soften. She appears visibly calmer after giving voice to her fear. I assure Sara that many people experience the same fear of being swallowed by darkness, and ask her to trust the process just a little longer. This time, Sara closes her eyes and sees an image of a lithe dancer moving in a strange, otherworldly landscape. "Could that be me?" she whispers. Tender tears begin to fall from the corners of her eyes as Sara reveals that she has secretly longed for years to take dance lessons but "I can't dance because my body is too big."

When Sara came into my office that day, she had been certain she was utterly empty and devoid of inspiration. Now Sara no longer knew what to think. She found it unsettling but also the beginning of a great new adventure. Over the next many months, Sara began the process of getting to know the mysterious part of herself that was *already* a dancer.

As you reach the outer limits of what you know—as the conscious mind releases control over the thinking process—you descend into the enigma of creation itself. Although you can read books, practice creativity exercises, and interview creators in order to gather information about the process of creativity, the single most important thing you can do to inspire yourself is, like Sara, to enter and discover your own mystery. Ask yourself: *Where might my creativity be hiding?*

······ · ··●

Every creative journey plunges us into mystery because we cannot know precisely where it will take us. Often, we fumble to find the words to describe the path, yet we can *sense* whether we are on it. Once the direction of our journey turns away from superficial preoccupations and tired patterns—and towards meaning and the essence of things—we can speak about creative expression as a *spiritual practice*.

Such *deep creativity* enables you to become more intimate with your authentic self, reunites you with your core values, and reveals how your own mystery connects to something more spacious, ecstatic, and transformative. When you bring this level of aliveness and healing to your work, you can create from a revitalized sense of meaning and wholeness.

All new things have their origin in darkness, in the inexpressible—beyond the reach of our own intellect. But so many of us worship the sun, basking in our outdoor gardens, distrustful of the night and the mystery that surrounds it. Yet all that beauty and blossoming abundance has sprung from darkness and remains rooted in its nourishing soil. Similarly, ideas and images emerge from the darkness of our being, like children emerging from the darkness of the womb. Out of mystery comes new life.

Further Reflections On Mystery

The painter Francis Bacon said, "The job of the artist is to deepen within the mystery." If you wish to go deeper, explore one or more of the following questions. *Write, draw, dance, paint, meditate . . .*

☞ As I recall an experience of mystery that led me to feel connected to something beyond myself, what sensations or feelings are present in my body? What are my thoughts about that experience? How might I communicate those feelings and thoughts?

☞ What keeps me connected to mystery? (Quiet contemplation? Listening to the song of a bird outside the kitchen window? Reading words of inspiration? Watching a sunset? Something else?) How do these experiences nourish my creative life? How might I give myself these experiences more often?

☞ What kind of fears do I experience when facing the unknown? Instead of letting fear stop me, how might I make use of the creative anxiety that resides at the heart of my dreams?

☞ How does my body feel when I overburden my creative soul with things and tasks in order to keep anxious uncertainty at bay?

☞ What are the deeper questions that compel my creative journey? How might I simplify my life to address these questions?

☞ How does my creative process nourish my spiritual life and vice versa?

☞ What are my ideas for exploring and communicating the mystery through my creative work?

*. . . And there were many times when I just wept
because I was releasing all this stuff about what had
to be. I let it all go . . . I knew something was coming,
and these losses were making room in my life for a
whole new possibility.*

—Sage Kimble

*My creative work has been the result of my grief, and
the source of my rebirth.*

—Dani Burch

Mourning

ONE OF THE SECRETS of creative work is knowing when the push into
outward activity needs to give way to receptive energies that draw us
down into ourselves—into feeling and being. As creators we are constantly grieving various sorts of losses: These are the "daily small deaths"
described by the dancer Martha Graham. We abandon many promising
directions to pursue a singular vision. We endure the humiliations and
pains of acquiring mastery. We attempt something new and it fails to
work the way we anticipated. We receive a rejection letter or we lose an
opportunity that goes to someone else. We destroy a piece of work that
fails to capture our intended vision. We abandon a previous success to
risk a new direction. Each of these occasions becomes a loss to mourn.

Let go, move on; let go, move on . . . is creativity's silent refrain.

If we have gone through our lives never mourning the big losses, we may not have enough internal capacity left to cope with the small daily losses that come with creative work.

Mourning is suffering with purpose.

In mourning, we acknowledge all that has come before this moment and all that must be relinquished before we can take the next step in a project or before we can reinvent ourselves. There is weight and, yes, pain, in mourning. But this kind of *necessary* pain can awaken a depth of passion and fortitude capable of launching you in a new direction.

······ꞏꞏ●

In the deepest experience of loss we all feel alone. But there is power and alchemical magic in such intensity of emotion. Once we allow ourselves to feel everything, the results can be life changing.

Let me tell a story, a very personal story. Confronting and sharing grief is about as personal as it gets. Here is what I remember.

I am thirty-seven and pregnant. I couldn't be happier. The timing is finally right. I have purposefully postponed motherhood in favor of creating a life of my own and acquiring a much needed sense of inner security which arrived quietly one day, almost as a benediction, after years of making my own way. I feel myself to be at the height of my powers, both personally and professionally. At last I feel ready—ready to be a mother, ready for the responsibility, ready to share my life. I am full of reckless hope about the future.

Weeks later, I wake up in the middle of the night feeling a sensation that belongs somewhere else. I lie very still, holding my legs together tight. My mind screams, "No! No!" But my body doesn't listen. Finally there is blood and I have this irrational desire to put it all back inside. A cold gust of wind howls through an open window. When the door slams, I feel myself to be a small thing in a dark cage.

······ꞏꞏ●

What do we grieve? Dreams that can never be fulfilled. Old ways of looking at the world, especially the tried and true methods of doing things that no longer work quite as well as they used to. Disappointments, betrayals, failures. Whatever expectations we're hanging onto—positive and negative—that fill us on the inside, but also prevent us from moving towards something new but as yet unseen. We may also mourn the passing of previous successes. Maybe we were once king of the hill or queen of the castle, but now we are trying to start over in a new place or another medium and so we feel like just another ant crawling on the ground.

In mourning, we let ourselves empty out.

I have stepped off the edge: Everything I have believed to be right and true has come apart at the very moment that it all seemed to be coming together. I feel as if I have ridden an elevator to the penthouse suite only to have it suddenly crash to the basement before I can step out and take in the view. I feel abandoned by everything in my life.

The loss of one baby, then another, and then my inability to conceive at all, brings an end to a dream that had waited patiently at the fringes of my life. I throw myself on the living room carpet crying out my anguish and rage. I feel betrayed by my body and by my own sense of moral responsibility. I have spent my prime childbearing years working with all my heart and soul to be a whole person for fear I might bequeath my mother's crippling emotional legacy to my own child. It has taken me such a long time to feel ready.

Now it is too late.

Why? Why? Why? But there is no answer. Just because . . . But why? Still, no answer. I fill in the blanks with my own bitterness. Because you are selfish. Because of your wild and misspent youth. Because you wasted so much time. Because you are thoughtless and undeserving. Because . . . Because . . . Because. If I can just keep filling the space with anger and answers, I won't have to feel the wreckage. And hovering right alongside the feeling of being irreparably damaged is a question so huge I can barely bring my consciousness to it: "What am I going to do with the rest of my life?" I rail at the unfairness of it all until I fall exhausted into bed. In the morning I awake to the sound of my own muffled sobbing.

······ ·· ●

If we are lucky, the sinking anguish of heartbreak softens us, inviting something unexpected to take over, flooding and filling us with sorrow, and eventually, with insight, hope, and shimmering optimism.

Months later, I accept an invitation to take a boat ride on the lake. In the waning days of Indian summer, crisp leaves curl in the dry heat, barely hanging on. The sky is big, the lake deserted. We float far far away from anywhere else. After a while, the silence brings me in too close—as if I can feel the earth slowing down. Everything seems to be dying or preparing to die. Bitter cold will be here soon. I shudder involuntarily.

A heron lifts off, her wings spread in graceful flight. I want to go with her. The click of the key and the roar of the engine comfort me. My spirit soars as the sky moves out in front of us . . . I am flying, fast and furious into forever. No death, not yet . . . Suddenly I am awash with gratitude. And I remember something I'd forgotten for a long time: I see my father's face. It is late and he is tired, and my father is making me lamb chops. The ordinary can sometimes astonish.

Quiet tears float behind my eyes. My chest threatens to explode. And I realize that I am experiencing something I've never felt before—unconditional acceptance. Not the idea of it—but an authentic total bodily expression—and the significance of the moment strikes me breathless with wonder . . .

In every act of creation, something dies so something new can be born. We imagine we can build our lives one piece at a time, holding on to each piece while acquiring the next, but even the most successful among us has discovered the hidden compromises and unexpected reversals of fortune that come with trying to have it all. Even with the arrival of a happy occasion, such as the birth of a child, we lose something. Parents relinquish their independence and the child gives up the security and safety of the womb. As soon as we move to embrace the excitement of possibility, we must also be prepared for the grief of letting go.

······ ··•

We have a hard time relinquishing the familiar. We collect and save, not only memorabilia, but also disappointments, betrayals, and ways of thinking about our lives that may not leave us much room for more creative options. These heirlooms bring comfort, but our habit of allowing them to define the present makes it difficult to experience fresh perspectives and interpretations.

Mourning permits us to break out of those tight, suffocating enclosures that keep us stuck in unproductive ways of thinking and behaving. Too often, we fear that if we let go, our lives will fall apart or we will discover that we are inept and unworthy. We may have to go through layers of cowardice and anger and shame; we may discover all manner of demeaning things about ourselves. But if we're willing to keep on going we'll find, underneath it all, something worth finding.

When the engine goes silent, quiet envelops us once again. We stare at the hills for a long time. All at once, I feel myself to be part of something more than what's in this world. And I remember something the spiritual activist Joanna Macy said: "The heart that breaks open can contain the whole universe." Grief can bring us to the edge of aliveness and communion if we allow it.

In the days, weeks, and months that followed this epiphany, a wondrous lucidity permitted me to live with a penetrating intuition. Although my body had lost its capacity to give birth, the very fact of this loss was somehow making it possible for me to discover something else that I never dreamed was within my capabilities.

While my physical being remained barren, my soul and spirit collaborated with a feverish urgency. The resulting surge of creative productivity culminated the following summer in the first exhibition of my pastel paintings. I will probably be coming to terms with the loss of motherhood for the rest of my life. But in opening fully to the injury, I can also appreciate the many satisfying ways that are available for me to give birth.

······ ··•

In the presence of significant loss, the mind's instinct for self-preservation cuts us off from the depth of our experience. Loss scares or embarrasses us, or we just don't know how to deal with all the pain that gets stirred up. With the passage of time, our conscious attention may be caught up once more in the momentum of living. But deep down, the wound still festers. Eventually, it starts growing long tentacles with voracious mouths that suck energy from every aspect of our lives. And the whole mess keeps on growing and mutating until one day we find that there's no room inside for anything new to germinate, no space for the energy of life. Left unattended, old pain paralyzes us, or turns us into busy robots, or makes us sick—mentally, physically, spiritually, or all three.

Sometimes the only way to re-inspire yourself—or to increase the stamina you need for dealing with everyday creative loss—is to face up to the previous losses that are stacked up behind it. Most creators incorporate loss into their work, either directly or indirectly. So if you're feeling spiritless, if your passion has deserted you, maybe it's time to do some grieving of your own.

Further Reflections On Mourning

The mindful mourning of your losses can transform them into sources of healing and inspiration. If you wish to go deeper, explore one or more of the following questions. *Write, draw, dance, paint, meditate . . .*

➤ What did I sacrifice to have the life I have now?

➤ In what ways am I still clinging to false hope for a life or conditions that can never be? Why am I refusing to allow this death or ending to occur?

➤ How does holding on to the past keep me from embracing new opportunity? When I imagine letting go, what do I feel in my body?

➤ What lessons have loss and sadness taught me? What capacities have I gained through suffering?

➤ How might I be diminishing myself by avoiding emotional pain?

➤ What losses and disappointments might I still need to grieve? What unfinished conversations from the past need completing?

➤ What is this sadness I cannot name? Can I take a moment and let it come forward? Where does hidden sadness sink roots inside my body? What if I draw my impression of it, or write a paragraph or two in a journal?

➤ When I feel bereft, what guides me back to the world?

☞ How might the creative process help me locate shards of light in my darkest hours?

☞ Can I recall a huge loss that may have helped me clarify what I care about? How did accepting it strengthen me?

☞ Imagine the storm has passed, washing me clean: What do I want? What new life am I moving into? What must I let go of? What must I accept?

☞ What loss might I be mourning in the future, if I don't act today?

Be patient toward all that is unsolved within your
heart and try to love the questions themselves.

—Rainer Maria Rilke

Humans are outraged when the supreme moments, the
moments of flowering, must be waited for . . .

—May Sarton

Patience and the mulberry leaf become a silk gown.

—Chinese proverb

Patience

THE CREATIVE PROCESS ASKS us not simply to fill an empty space, but to enter it and wait. While our ideas may come to us in a flash of inspiration, patience readies them for the world. Sometimes we have an idea but it's really just a germ of an idea, a flicker that crosses our mind. We don't always understand it fully. We make a quick sketch or scribble some notes, but it's not fully fleshed out. Meanwhile, we must wait. Some insights break through into conscious awareness in hours, others in weeks or months. Still others may take years to ripen.

The lack of patience can be costly. Once a man found a cocoon nestled in the bark of a tree. He watched for a while as the butterfly slowly worked to create a hole. Impatient for results, he decided to help the butterfly and tore open the cocoon. The butterfly emerged intact—however, it was not quite fully developed. As the butterfly attempted to take flight, its crumpled wings remained stuck to its body. After waging a desperate struggle, the butterfly dropped to its death.

As creators, we do much to injure our own wings when we run roughshod over the gradual unfolding of our process. If we fail to allow our ideas—not to mention our courage, skills, and endurance—to ripen of their own accord, we may push and prod our dreams to their untimely death. If, out of impatience, we continuously force ourselves to attempt what we are not ready to do, we will become more timid. Instead of using our mind and energy to explore the unknown and risk new directions, we will find ways to avoid anticipated pressures. In the creative process, everything must come of itself and in its own time. As the poet Rumi reminds us, "Everything is gestation and bringing forth." Ask yourself: *Is there something I am currently struggling with that may need a little more time to grow into itself?*

·····˙··•

In the creative process, practicing patience means recognizing that we are still learning, still evolving, while moving, sometimes imperceptibly, toward growing our work. In an age of instant gratification and quick fixes, patience asks us to cultivate a long-term view of our creative lives, reserve judgment, persevere, and not get too attached to any one outcome or circumstance.

Whenever I need reminding that a creator's reality continuously evolves, I think of this story.

Once upon a time, there was an old farmer who had worked his crops for many years. One day his horse ran away. Upon hearing the news, his neighbors came to visit. "Such bad luck," they said sympathetically. "We shall see," the farmer replied. The next morning the horse returned, bringing with it three other wild horses. "How wonderful," the neighbors exclaimed. "We shall see," replied the old man.

The following day, his son tried to ride one of the untamed horses, was thrown, and broke his leg. The neighbors again came to commiserate. "We shall see," answered the farmer. The day after, military officials came to the village to conscript young men into the army. Seeing that the son's leg was broken, they passed him by. Once again, the neighbors gathered to congratulate the farmer on his good fortune. "We shall see," replied the farmer . . .

When working on a project, we can never be sure if things will go right . . . or wrong. Just at the moment a project seems to be coming together, it may fail to gel. Just when we feel frustration and panic are about to convince us we will never find the solution, an elegant answer may call out from the chaos. We may lose an important contract, but six weeks later, a former client calls with a commission we didn't expect. Cultivating a "we shall see" attitude frees us to focus our efforts in the moment, making them as authentic as possible.

Of course we also need to be proactive about results. Setting goals, making lists, and following action plans are important organizational tools for ensuring success. It's just that we need to balance our passion for outcomes with the limits of our ability to control them. Our creations sometimes seem to have minds of their own—ask any novelist. Certainly, our own minds are split and conflicted. And let's not forget the unforeseeable impacts of other people's agendas on our progress. As creators, our efforts and experiences have deep value that cannot be found in the frantic pursuit of end products. Patience reminds us to find fulfillment in the process itself.

······˙··●

Sometimes I become so frustrated by all the problems and complications involved in bringing this book to life that I find myself straining through the process as if struggling to grasp a sweet reward that is just beyond my reach. I want so badly to be done—to see the words I've poured my heart out over in their beautifully designed and bound package. That's when I need to take a breath and choose balance over forced results. At the heart of patience lies acceptance. I know I'll get there—eventually.

Opportunities for learning patience abound in our day-to-day lives. We can practice patience while waiting for a tardy friend or our dawdling kids; while standing in line at the market or bank; while waiting for someone to finish talking so we can have a turn; while stuck in traffic or when that "idiot" cuts in front of us. And don't get me started on my unbelievably slow Internet connection. *Grumpf!*

Nowhere, however, is the practice of patience more essential, more humbling, and more challenging than when we experience a life-changing event that requires us to question the way we have previously lived. Nothing gets us more riled up than a life interrupted—especially when it comes to our working, producing lives.

Several years ago, I had a client whose high-powered success depended to a large degree on her ability to pressure situations into conforming to her expectations. An accomplished lawyer, Sondra also served on the board of an international scholarship fund. In addition to her many responsibilities, she managed to find the time to paint and occasionally exhibit her paintings. Sondra was a mover and a shaker. If a tough job needed doing, she found a way to get it done. Like most of us, her strength was also her weakness: The tension required to keep performing at such a high level finally resulted in physical injury.

On a typically crazed morning, Sondra dashed around the bedroom, zipping up her skirt while talking on the phone. Stretching up to a high shelf for her favorite pair of Manolos, Sondra extended her reach beyond what her fifty-year-old body could tolerate. And then, "I felt a terrible tear."

In an instant, Sondra's life changed. Although she didn't realize it at the time, she had crossed an intangible threshold and begun an irreversible journey. And she would need all the patience she could muster to complete it.

Following a brief period of rest, Sondra attempted to resume her former life. But after a while, she had to admit, "I'm not getting any better." Unrelenting physical pain forced Sondra to confront her impatience in a way that nothing else could. No matter what Sondra's mind commanded, her body could no longer tolerate being pushed. The "incident," as she euphemistically referred to it, eventually turned into a classic midlife struggle with her soul. In order to heal her body, Sondra needed to live within the limits of her changing circumstances. At first, Sondra was incensed. "It's not fair," she complained.

·······•

Moving from one state of being to another is difficult—whether we are transitioning from healthy to sick, overweight to fit and trim, single to married, able-bodied to injured, worker to retiree, addict to recovering addict, child-free to new parent, struggling artist to exhibiting artist, or writer to author. Any time we evolve from one identity to another, we must traverse a great divide of uncertainty. This is a place of mystery because we are no longer what we were, and we are not yet who we will become. We humans don't like uncertainty. Transitions can often be long phases when it feels like we are waiting for something, although we don't necessarily know what. Waves of anxiety may engulf us at different transition points in our lives, or even during different phases of creative work on a single project.

Crossing the great divide between the two worlds of what *was* and what *will be* takes skill and patience. The mysterious universe of Sondra's undiscovered life beckoned. Whatever was in store, Sondra needed to heal more than just her physical body. She needed to relax the rigidity and perfectionism that had served her professionally—and had, in no small measure, sheltered her vulnerability beneath an impenetrable shield of formidability. Now that her body had rebelled, Sondra felt inept, frightened, confused—and angry.

Creating a new way of life would require Sondra to redefine herself beyond the things she could control. Reluctantly, Sondra set out to cultivate a new respect for the gifts that her vulnerability could offer. Her life would be different, but it could be just as satisfying. Our work together helped Sondra ease into the darkness of her unexplored inner life. As she learned to wait, without letting anxiety pull her away, Sondra could finally hear the soundless voice of her heart. Through patient and conscientious exploration, Sondra began moving toward the future that awaited her.

For personalities like Sondra, who are used to taking the bull by the horns, waiting is sometimes the most efficient way to go about solving a problem. Hyperactivity is actually one way of resisting the natural cycles of fullness, fading, and emptiness that characterize creative work, as well as the process of healing. Futile attempts to force solutions will only create a block where none exists. One might as well try directing the waxing and waning of the moon or command the movement of the tides. Ask yourself: *How patient can I be with uncertainty?*

·······•

We are an impatient nation of get-up-and-goers. Our strength lies in our energy and enthusiasm for action. The breath of inspiration inflates our sails and off we go, flying with the wind. Consumed by the energy of work and the rush of possibilities, we expect that this state of flow should continue indefinitely, and when it doesn't, we become alarmed.

In every project, as in every life, there comes a point when we need to take it one step further but we don't know what that one step is. Or we do take a step and the new ground gives out from under us. Anxiety mounts as we struggle to control a situation that has clearly gone beyond our conscious control.

The real process of creation begins only after this outburst of energy subsides—after we have run out of ideas, ambition, and a sense of direction. When we begin to feel uncertain, empty, confused, lost, or overwhelmed—when we don't know where to turn, follow the advice of the poet Rainer Rilke. It is time to be patient; it is time to "live the questions."

Patience permits us to step away from the problem and release our anxious exertions. We relinquish control to the unconscious mind, where various possibilities need time to incubate before they can emerge, like a butterfly, into the light of consciousness.

A large part of developing patience is having faith in yourself that eventually, you will get there. Even though you may want to fly right away, your secret, vulnerable places need to go slow. Learn to be patient and respect what is unsettled within yourself. It doesn't matter whether you are moving on from a life-changing event, or whether you are struggling to take your work to the next level. Give yourself time and space to grow into your aspirations. With a little patience you might even surprise yourself.

Further Reflections On Patience

Your creative goals may be inspired by *passion*, but they can only be achieved with *patience*. If you wish to go deeper, explore one or more of the following questions. *Write, draw, dance, paint, meditate . . .*

☞ What do I notice when I feel the sensations of impatience? (Anxiety?

Tension? Anger? Shortness of breath?) At what point does frustration overwhelm me? Does my impatience support my creativity or undermine it?

☙ What can I do when I first notice the internal tension and judgmental thoughts that signal impatience? (Might slowing my breath and focusing on my senses—hearing, seeing, smelling, tasting, and touching—help me feel more patient?)

☙ How can I hold my vision of the future while staying focused on where I am in the process? What have I already achieved even as I await the next unfolding?

☙ Is it difficult for me to be patient with certain phases of creative work or during transitional periods in my life—those times when nothing is certain or secure? What am I afraid of?

☙ What have I waited for with positive results?

☙ How can the practice of patience renew my connection to what is most essential and enduring?

☙ What might I discover if I sat in front of a single painting for two hours?

Trust, not assurance, glides us past what we know,
enabling us to tumble into the new.

—Peter London

Our mightiest ally is belief in something we cannot
see, hear, touch, taste, or feel.

—Stephen Presfield

Trust your own experience. Trust your own values
and your own needs.

—Esther Myers

Trust

"IS THE UNIVERSE A FRIENDLY PLACE?"

Albert Einstein posed this deceptively simple question, which has profound ramifications for creators who must navigate the sprawling periods of incomprehension that characterize creative work. The ability to trust, even more than passion or talent, influences not only our experience of the creative journey, but also the levels of stamina and resilience we can muster in order to complete it—or even if we can complete it at all.

Why does the capacity to trust exert so much leverage over a creator's fate? Much of creation begins with an act of trust. Depending on your working style, you may dive into creative work without knowing where you are headed. But even when you have a clear vision of your destination, it's not as if you can google for directions. You can only take one step at a time and wait for the next right action to suggest itself.

Although creative work sometimes feels lonely, we are never truly alone. We carry with us the unconscious imprint of all we have gleaned from prior encounters with trust and uncertainty. If you answer Einstein's query in the affirmative, and experience the universe as a friendly place, you will probably feel less anxious and more self-assured while traversing the vagaries of a creative life than someone who suffered early experiences of abandonment, abuse, or neglect. But even if you had a relatively secure start in life, your temperament or upbringing may not predispose you to navigating the ups and downs of creative uncertainty. Ask yourself: *Can I trust the unseen?*

For creators who are determined to heal, the creative process offers a profound opportunity to rebuild a shaky foundation of trust. You may need to take the time to remember and relive those earliest betrayals. But consciously immersing yourself in your wounds—with the all-important intention of healing—will move you beyond wallowing to an enlarged capacity for trust and, eventually, an increased tolerance for the risk-taking required to achieve your dreams.

······•

What does it mean to trust? Trust flows from two fundamental beliefs. If we believe in ourselves, then we can depend on our inner resourcefulness to carry us through difficulty. And if we also believe we are connected to forces of creativity operating beyond our own consciousness, then we feel partnered with the Universe. Trusting the creative process frequently means following promptings we may not fully understand but are willing to honor.

When I first moved from Los Angeles—an urban funhouse filled with varied and infinite diversions—I had already built the beginnings of an innovative business amidst the hustle and bustle of city life. I did

not fully understand the insistent call that compelled me to leave everything familiar behind and move, by myself, to what was then a sleepy
little town in rural northern California . . .

*After the first couple of days in my tiny one-room studio, I find myself
standing at a pay phone on a dusty corner, tears streaming down my face,
frantically calling everyone I know back home. Instead of comfort, I receive
the cold recordings of answering machines. Apparently my friends are out on
the town and carrying on with their lives without me.*

For the moment, I have lost whatever modicum of trust brought me here.

*I hang up the phone and stand staring out at an abandoned market, paint
peeling off the siding. A faded red and white sign advertising GROUND
BEEF SPECIAL droops sideways in the window. There are no cars; a stray
newspaper swirls past on a sudden gust. My solitude feels too terrifying
to bear. Everything in the world seems to be either lost or leaving. I wish I
could press a button and jettison myself out of this place. Instead, I walk
the quiet country roads for hours, eventually finding my way back to my
new home.*

*Despite the tangled mass of contradictions churning in my body, I refuse
to go back. Whatever happens, I will remain faithful to my call. I have
created space around me: I am determined to use it to discover things about
myself; I am determined to create a more nourishing life. Despite palpable
despair, I carry an expectant sense of possibility. I trust my inner knowingness,
whispering instructions, and imploring me to stay the course. I trust whatever
has led me here and whatever wants to express itself through me—and I
trust that it will not let me fall . . .*

I am much older now. I can tell you today that I regard that move as
the single best decision of my life. But it took years of hard work before
I actually started to *see* and *feel* the positive results of that decision. At
the time, I had no idea how the move would turn out. We may work for
a long time without any clear evidence that the journey is worth the

effort and sacrifice. Trust and perseverance are the qualities that see us through until we have tangible proof that our instincts are correct.

·····˙··●

I feel so hopeless when it seems like nothing is happening. Uncertainty can stir up dark places within the psyche. Once trust gives way to despondency, it's tempting to give up on ourselves and our dreams. When it comes to navigating the creative process *knowledge is power*—particularly when we have come to the limits of trust. Even if our capacity to trust rests on shaky ground, educating ourselves about the *miracle of incubation* and the workings of the unconscious mind may help nervous creators stave off the impulse to cut and run.

Incubation is a stage during the process when the unconscious mind holds the problem without expending any conscious energy to solve it. The question may hang on the periphery, or retreat entirely out of sight. Protected from the prying eyes (and judgments) of conscious attention, fledgling ideas and potential solutions float, swirl, and eventually connect in new ways. Meanwhile, we must go on about our business, living our lives as best we can within the ongoing uncertainty. "Living the questions," as the poet Rumi advises, means trusting the creative process as it works within us.

How can I find refuge in uncertainty? By allowing the questions to flow through you into the shadows. By living with the edges of confusion and doubt. By breathing. By walking in the darkness. Soon you will pick up a brush or a pen, or you will sit at a potter's wheel, or you will place your fingers on the piano. Let the paint, the words, the clay, the music—the very movement of your body—speak for you. Trust the waiting inside that can't yet be named.

·····˙··●

As creators, we must learn to place our faith in the unconscious processes that precede periods of productivity, which, in turn, give rise to tangible recognizable outcomes. Once we have run out of ideas and solutions, we have no choice but to trust the unconscious mind to do the work that the conscious mind cannot perform.

If this all sounds rather abstract, let's talk about something we all can relate to—dessert.

Do you enjoy baking from scratch? Well, baking is one of my hobbies. It's a great way to relax and yet accomplish something at the same time, plus it makes people happy. There's nothing like a slice of sweet indulgence to restore my faith that all is right with the world. As luck would have it, the process of baking *also* happens to be a gentle metaphor for trusting the creative unconscious.

Whenever I decide to try something new, I relish the process of researching recipes. If I want to make a coconut cream cake, like I just did for my sister's Big Zero birthday, I will browse through ten or twenty coconut cream cake recipes (so easy to do on the Internet these days). Once I have saturated myself with words and images of sweet, creamy goodness, I am positively salivating with anticipation. That's how I know it's time to close the screen and make the mashup my own. Next, I buy the highest quality ingredients and mix them all together.

Ok, so far I am conscious and in control of what I am doing—not much trust is required.

But once I put the whole concoction in the oven, it's out of my hands. And if I am trying something new, this is where I start to get a little nervous. I have no idea whether the final product will turn out the way I imagined. At this point, I need to trust I've done the best I can. I release the batter into the care of the oven. From there, I must trust them both. If I trust the oven to keep a constant temperature, the gooey mixture will rise, take shape, solidify, and brown. The ingredients will re-form themselves through the magic of chemistry, emerging at the appointed time, transformed from what they were when I brought them together. Meanwhile, I'll go outside and repot that root-bound plant I've been neglecting—which is really another way of saying, "Don't hover."

When I first started baking, I can't tell you how many goodies I ruined by opening the door every ten minutes because I just couldn't calm the feeling that I had to check up on things. I ended up sabotaging the process with all my anxious poking and prodding.

The same principle applies when it comes to our ideas. We need to trust the unconscious process of incubation to turn the swirling vagaries of thought and feeling into a coherent form without our force of will. Hypervigilance may come in handy in a war zone, or when you're strolling down a blind alley on a moonless night, but when it comes to creativity, too much vigilance will disrupt your process. It really comes down to managing your feeling of urgency so that you don't end up panicking and collapsing whatever's "incu-baking" (sorry, I couldn't resist) in your oven.

······˙··●

Conflict and uncertainty are an integral part of the creative process. We struggle and sometimes even suffer. Trust helps us make it through to the other side. We build confidence by engaging with the experience of uncertainty. Often we don't trust our creativity because we don't go deep enough to truly test ourselves. When we skim along the surface of life, we continually move on to something new, even before we have seriously explored what we have. When we habitually ignore our deepest sensibilities—keeping ourselves stuck in deadening habits, patterns, and choices because it feels safe—we lack the foundation on which to create anything of real personal value.

The practice of trust does not require the absence of *mistrust*. Rather, we choose to trust based on the recognition that we can find meaning and fulfillment in challenging ourselves to deepen beyond the boundaries of the familiar. Trust does not require passive acceptance or blind faith. When we trust, we actively engage with our fears, insecurities, and limitations. Like Dante, in the fourteenth-century epic poem *The Divine Comedy*, or the high priestess, Inanna, in the ancient Sumerian descent myth, we too leave behind familiar touchstones and competencies as the creative journey drives us into the underworld of the unconscious. As we descend further and further into our psychological core, we reconnect to the primal power of our passions by peeling away the layers of conditioning, betrayal, and false identity. With each and every encounter, we gain valuable insight and strength, until eventually, when we least expect it, we find ourselves standing in the light, shaken, but transformed beyond the limitations of our former identity.

Going deep teaches us that vulnerability can expand and enlarge our self-confidence. In the face of such a harrowing descent, fidelity to the journey salves our wounds of mistrust. Once trust joins with perseverance, it solidifies the ground beneath a creator's feet. *Trust* says, "Yes, this is difficult. You need to stop and learn some new things right now, but I'll be with you every step of the way."

Further Reflections On Trust

Author Gregg Levoy advises creators: "Go towards the things that are beckoning at the deepest levels, and the rest will take care of itself." If you wish to go deeper, explore one or more of the following questions. *Write, draw, dance, paint, meditate . . .*

☞ In what ways do I withdraw from creative challenges because of an uncertain outcome?

☞ Can I make a list of the important experiences that affected my ability to trust and then narrow the list down to those few experiences that bring up the sharpest emotional sting? What is the current impact of these previous betrayals? How can I heal? Who can support me in restoring my capacity to trust?

☞ What habitual assumptions about myself and others do I make that may prevent me from trusting?

☞ Where does my need to have things go according to plan get in the way of being able to navigate the ups and downs of the creative process?

☞ Under what circumstances am I most likely to doubt myself?

☞ What would I create if I trusted in my gifts and purpose? What inner capacities might I count on to see me through creative challenges? What protections, fears, beliefs, or habits might I release?

☞ In what ways have I learned to trust because I have grown from past mistakes?

☞ What restores me to a sense of trust? (Exhilarating physical activity? A calming yoga class? Reading words that inspire and inform? A weekend retreat in nature? The company of a good friend who engages me in a meaningful discussion about my creative work? Volunteering in the community? Something else?)

*We must learn to become less attached to what
we think we ought to know. . . . And more deeply
committed to the emergence of that which wants
to be known through and within us.*

—Beverly-Colleene Galyean

*It is by logic that we prove, but
by intuition that we discover.*

—Henri Poincaré

Think with your whole body.
—Taisen Deshimaru

Intuition

I HAD AN EERIE EXPERIENCE this morning. I went running along the bluff
trail that passes a few steps from the sprawling white canvas of a house
I have come to think of as home. I've been making regular sojourns to
this quiet coastal community where I can write undisturbed while
the sounds of the ocean serenade my soul. Usually, I stay inside and
hunker down in front of the computer on overcast days; but my head
was filled with sticky, anxious thoughts from the moment I woke up,
and I was hoping to jump-start some new ones.

Heading out under a canopy of soft grey clouds, my feet find a
familiar rhythm, my breathing slows and deepens, as cool ionized air
suffuses my lungs. I hum along, tripping the light fantastic, when I find
myself suddenly slowing for no particular reason—except that I feel my
intuition pulling my body off the main path and towards the distant

outline of a woman slowly moving in my direction. We stop to share a casual greeting. An odd feeling of familiarity arises, although we do not recognize each other. The sea breezes begin whipping at our bare legs so we step behind a bank of brush to continue our conversation. After a few more minutes, we find an explanation for our feeling of connection: We once met in college through mutual friends—almost forty years ago.

During the creative process, we do certain things and feel drawn to other things without really understanding why. Intuition helps us to find our way. Creators receive important information—clues—through the portal of the body. While our five senses (sight, smell, taste, touch, and hearing) help us gather information from the *outside-in*, our intuition asks us to pay attention to what is happening from the *inside-out*.

Intuition may present as a hunch, a sudden idea, a musical tone, an image, a dream, a voice, a sensation, or an impulse we can't really explain—like the impulse that caused me to slow my pace while running along the bluff trail. My intuition turned me in a different direction so I could make an unexpected connection.

Sometimes intuition strikes suddenly. In such instances, we feel overcome by a feeling that something is not only essential, but right and . . . inevitable. At other times, intuition gently nudges us in a direction that may all too easily be overlooked in the daily hustle of our information-overloaded lives. As creators, we must come to recognize guidance that speaks to us from our depths. We must, as the poet Rilke counsels, "go deep . . . to find the anonymous and multiple rhythms of the blood."

······˙··●

Einstein, no slouch when it came to matters of the intellect, respected *intuition* as a "sacred gift" and *rationality* as its "faithful servant." While acknowledging the indispensable part each performs in the creative process, he believed that Western culture had gotten their roles backwards: "Our society reveres the servant and has forgotten the gift."

Promptings from intuition come to us through the intimacy of the body, which is precisely the reason they are considered suspect. The phrase "just a feeling," speaks volumes about how little respect we give our inner life. But the reasoning mind is not the only path to knowledge. Feeling is a kind of knowing too.

The body remembers what the mind forgets.
The body knows before the mind comprehends.
The body speaks without words;
The mind uses words
to claim the throne and conquer the kingdom.

Intuition does not explain, but simply points the way. Don't ask your intuition to justify itself by providing proof; it isn't interested in detail. The rational mind likes to know what is going on at all times. How else can it run the show? Its power comes from *naming*. What cannot be named disturbs and then disrupts. The whisper of nuanced wisdom doesn't give the rational mind the satisfaction of feeling solidly in charge. Instead, despite intuition's ring of truth, there remains a profusion of doubts about how this felt-impression is going to play out in real time.

······•

The conscious rational mind and its consort, the ego, don't like to hand over the keys to the kingdom, or even contemplate sharing them, especially with something as imprecise as *feeling*. It is a matter of pride. And power. Our culture tends to discount the value of "knowing without knowing how we know," in favor of training, technique, and formal education that focus primarily on left-brain skills.

I was born into a family where book learning and intellectual knowledge were valued above all other kinds of knowing. Reasoning, being smart, knowing things—especially being able to *measure* or *prove* what you know—mattered a great deal. There was no respect for the tentative, ambiguous, heartfelt ways of navigating life. Like many creative people, I was born feeling life through my body. I didn't learn until many years later that I had inherited the "highly sensitive" trait described by Dr. Elaine Aron in her book *The Highly Sensitive Person*.

Growing up, I felt certain something was wrong with me. My responses were emotional and exaggerated compared with how easily others seemed to roll with the punches. Everything affected me deeply. With effort, I learned to be analytical, like my father, but as successful as I was at emulating him, ultimately there was no denying I had inherited my mother's hyper-sensitive nature. I felt deeply ashamed of my inability to separate myself from my feelings. I spent much of my early life trying to control and intellectualize the seemingly incomprehensible flood of sensation that bombarded me daily. As a result, I lost confidence in my creative instincts.

Many blocked creators believe they aren't creative. Frequently, the problem is just the opposite. Natural intuitives possess an innate ability to process sensory data much more deeply and thoroughly than others. But without support, training, and the all-important skills for self-nurturing, the nervous system shuts down to prevent sensory overload. Once we turn the volume down, move out of our bodies, and take up permanent residence in the pragmatic, rational mind, we can no longer attend to the subtle signals that drive the creative process. Ask yourself: *Could this be me? Am I innately sensitive but over-protecting myself to the point that I have lost contact with my natural intuitive abilities?*

·······´··•

Many people experience intuition's heightened receptivity as a profound state of grace, which is perhaps why Einstein referred to it as
"a sacred gift." From a spiritual perspective, intuition is a felt-moment
outside of ordinary time during which we experience ourselves as
intertwined with the mysterious forces of creation itself. A continuous
exchange of information takes place at a wordless level in the form of
energy—between us and everything around us—whether we are consciously aware of it or not. Most of us spend so much time distracting
ourselves or using our analytical mind to figure out things that we are
simply not aware of at the subliminal levels of body consciousness.

The body's nervous system operates like an antenna. It both sends
and receives energy. Our intuition uses this "energy data," as the medical
intuitive Caroline Myss refers to it, to make decisions in the present
moment. Once we sense the promptings of the intuitive self seamlessly
intertwined with guidance from the Universe, we gain creative freedom.
As receptive creators become one with the mysterious, intangible forces
of creation, a way forward suggests itself. Meanwhile, our mere mortal
selves stand apart, astonished as to how we hadn't seen such obvious
implications in the first place.

·····´··•

*I am pretty bound up in my rational mind. How can I develop my
intuition?* The best way to develop your intuition is to pay attention to
what moves beneath the surface of your skin. If you have been told your
entire life that you are "too sensitive," now is the chance to fine-tune and
channel your natural intuitive abilities.

If an image comes to you on a walk, ask it a question. If you are
taking a hot shower and a voice inside speaks to you, listen. If you rise

up in the middle of the night in a cold sweat, ask yourself: "What am I afraid of?" If flecks of light bouncing off the water move you to tears, paint them. If you are too tired to care, ask: "Who has abandoned me in the past?" If you overhear a conversation at Starbucks and your ears start to burn, write it down. Develop a habit of checking in with your intuition by asking: "Does this feel right?" Practice acting on small hunches and keep track of how they turn out. You can count on intuition to bring you what you need if you are willing to meet it halfway.

······ ··●

Creativity emerges from different levels of thought and feeling. The raw energy of the creative unconscious seeks its own path, like a meandering river; the conscious rational mind controls its structure, direction, and timing like a project manager. Intuition becomes the bridge of communication between the two minds.

When we grapple with complex issues, we often do not have enough knowledge in our rational mind to move forward. We attempt to force solutions we reason will work, but often these solutions don't connect to our core. We *think* they will work. Maybe we even feel they *should* work because they worked in the past for us, or for a friend. Maybe these solutions even appear to meet the criteria on our checklists. Take for example dating the seemingly perfect partner who meets all our parameters, but with whom we ultimately can't get comfortable. Frequently, ideal solutions don't necessarily fit for us, even though we're at a loss to explain why.

To move past the standoff between our personal agendas—between our *idea* of what is true or what we *want* to be true—and the *resonance* of intuitive truth, we must let go of our relentless worry and analysis. Intuition liberates the creator from the paralysis of over-thinking. Anything that takes us out of our thinking mind, including processes such as drawing, listening to music, meditation, movement, or a guided imagery session—or just taking a hot bath or shooting a game of pool—can help move the point of our attention away from the preoccupations of a clenched, worried mind, while slowly coaxing cryptic communications from the deep.

Many of us feel uncomfortable with the language of the body, with all its messy whirl of sensation and emotion. We prefer to think. But the kind of thinking that won't allow itself to be guided by feeling becomes shortsighted, tedious, and uninspired. At worst, it leads to cold calculation, arrogant superiority, and strategic manipulation rather than authenticity.

Intuition breathes life into the structure of technique and the discipline of training. What we know instinctively, without being taught, elevates inspired creators. When we allow ourselves to be guided by what the poet Ralph Waldo Emerson called "the primary wisdom" of intuition, our ideas germinate and bloom and our creations become infused with an authenticity and aliveness that will bring others alive as well.

Further Reflections On Intuition

Develop a habit of continually checking in with your intuition by asking yourself: Does this feel right to me? If you wish to go deeper, explore one or more of the following questions. *Write, draw, dance, paint, meditate . . .*

☞ How does knowledge that arises from *instinct* differ from knowledge that arises from a *rational* process? Where do I connect with each kind of knowledge in my body?

☞ When do I *act* on my gut feelings and when do I *wait* until all the facts speak for themselves?

☞ How can I distinguish between the pull of my personal agenda and the subtle resonance of intuition?

☞ How does intuitive insight get my attention? (As a hunch? As a dream? As an image? As music? Through my body, as a feeling or sensation? As a sudden bright idea? While reading a passage in a book, or hearing a song or a snatch of overheard conversation that really hits home?)

☞ How have I used intuitive information in the past?

☞ When do my emotions and thoughts become so strong that they overwhelm the subtlety of my intuition?

☞ How does it feel in my body when I suspend judgment and accept data that doesn't make sense in the moment, or that cannot be applied immediately?

☞ What practices help me unwind and center myself?

☞ When my intuition alerts me to something I don't want to know, how do I work through my objections in order to accept felt-truth?

I have begun listening to the teachings
my blood whispers to me.

—*Herman Hesse*

Making the work you want to make means finding
nourishment within the work itself.

—David Bayles and Ted Orland

Work is love made visible.
—Kahlil Gibran

The artist is nothing without the gift.
The gift is nothing without work.

—Émile Zola

5
Working
Passionately

INALLY IT'S TIME TO GET TO WORK! Everything we have
done up to now has prepared us for illumination and the
period of creative productivity that follows. Through the
consciously initiated processes of defining purpose, exploring, learning,
concentrating, and deepening we have readied ourselves to receive
answers from the mystery.

As new understanding, images, and ideas break through into
conscious awareness, the creatures of the dark dissolve into the light of
liberation. Seized by this sense of freedom, we plunge into creative work
filled with the breath of inspiration ("Aha!") and newfound direction.

To work with passion means so much more than making a tangible
product. "True art strikes deeper than the surface," wrote artist Robert
Henri. Our creations rise to the level of *art* when imbued with soul.
And to put our soul into what we do transforms drudgery into a labor
of love.

The ecstasy found at the heart of passionate work is a peculiar combination of anxiety and joy. Ecstasy results from the powerful but contradictory forces within us—the chaotic intensity of intuitive flow and the need to order and channel that energy into form. The best creative work unifies this duality in the expression of a vital truth. Products of such a dynamic struggle go beyond mere technical achievement—their elegance and beauty resonate with a universal understanding that reaches out to others in silent homage.

To work with passion inevitably involves a dance with contradiction. Creators experience fluctuating periods of lucid absorption and confusion, doubt and confidence, intensity and relaxation. The romantic poet John Keats described the capacity to embrace this internal complexity without trying to resolve the contradictions as *negative capability*. A creator's mind needs to be a "thoroughfare for all thought," wrote Keats. Such intellectual receptivity allows the flow of uncensored ideas and feelings to find expression through art. The task of integrating our own internal contradictions becomes one of the primary challenges of creative work.

Passionate work responds to the whole human being, unifying our practical and poetic natures. When you encounter inevitable periods of frustration, focus on the deeper purpose of your work. Are you working to complete a task, find a means of escape, earn money, garner personal recognition, or discover and express deeper values? Ask yourself: *What fundamental purpose drives my creative work?*

Qualities that shape passion into great work include *clarity, engagement, tension, consistency,* and *rest*.

Clarity shines a light on solutions that inform and inspire the work. *Engagement* secures our total absorption and connection to the work. *Tension* fuels the creative transformation from vision to reality. *Consistency* shows up for work despite doubts and distractions. *Rest* restores the creative spirit, replenishing vital mental and emotional energies.

In this exalted state I can see clearly
what is obscure in my ordinary moods.

—Johannes Brahms

The AHA! moment is often a place you weren't
expecting to be—a mistake.

—Eric Rodenbeck

To see what is in front of one's nose
needs a constant struggle.

—George Orwell

Clarity

HAVE YOU EVER FORGOTTEN SOMETHING you were about to say and given up in exasperation, only to have the elusive information pop back into your mind from out of nowhere? Or while picking over tomatoes at the market (thinking about nothing in particular), do you recall having been struck by a resolution to a quandary you had been wrestling with for several weeks? The solution suddenly appears so obvious, you wonder why it took so long to figure out.

The unconscious problem-solving mechanism that initiates these everyday examples of spontaneous recognition also helps creators move their work forward. The information that comes during a state of creative clarity may hit all at once, like a flash of lightning, or flow into us like a stream running free. At other times, clarity dawns subtly at the fringes of awareness. In whatever way we experience it, clarity provides internal illumination—a moment of grace when everything that has been previously imagined, learned, and digested comes together.

Whenever I am in the midst of a creative struggle, clarity announces herself as a subtle vibration of energy, a quickening that rises up from the depths and radiates throughout my entire body. I can scarcely contain the desire to express everything that has been patiently held for so long—answers, direction, and inspiration flood my mind with a startling urgency. Working within the energy of clarity brings a delicious pleasure—a sort of spiritual food—filling the once empty places with a special radiance. The joy of creative work comes from this lucidity of purpose and energetic immediacy—as much as the completion of a project.

·····ʾ··●

The breakthrough of ideas or images following periods of confusion and struggle can be one of the most invigorating of all human experiences. The phenomenon is a literal meeting of the minds as the *conscious* mind becomes aware of what the *unconscious* mind has secretly processed. Richer and more powerful than knowledge gleaned through rational analysis, the joining of our two minds brings *a kind of knowing that is felt and understood simultaneously*. Sudden clarity resonates as truth because it feels essential. The penetrating quality of deep insight confirms a sense of inner strength and a feeling of rightness that enables us to say, "I realize something important."

·····ʾ··●

Once we have realized something important, are we willing to accept and act on it? My client Maria has a highly imaginative temperament. On a daily basis, her innovative personality expresses itself in a delightfully eccentric sense of style. From time to time, Maria brings me pieces of experimental projects—hand-painted fabric, drawings of whimsical cats that she intends to make into cards, one-of-a-kind gift-wrapped boxes, or stunning still-life arrangements inside shadow boxes. At other times, Maria talks about singing lessons, film making, and becoming an actress. All of it has potential, but none of it ever goes very far. She certainly doesn't lack for ideas. Like most of us, she has plenty of them.

Maria has a problem many would envy. Her close-knit family provides for all her needs. She works at the family business, socializes with members of her large extended clan, and rents a cozy cottage at a reduced rate from her aunt. Despite so much security, Maria feels frustrated and empty "living a life that was chosen *for* me."

During our meetings, Maria connects with her innate competence and sets her sights on a course of action. She tells me that she needs to move away from the enveloping security her family provides in order to pursue her own vision. But in between our sessions, Maria distances herself from that moment of clarity, retreating into the practiced habits and familiar dramas of dependency.

Clarity opens the door to accountability. The special insight that is clarity's gift may frequently suggest a course of action you are reluctant to take. If you fear the consequences of this new knowledge, you may turn away from whatever inspired truth has been revealed. The Brazilian lyricist and novelist Paulo Coelho echoes this notion. "It is particularly difficult to accept that you know what you're supposed to do when you are not doing it." Because from the moment that you know the truth, you have to either leave a lot of things behind or live aware that you are not honoring yourself at a fundamental level.

Deep down, Maria longs to spread her wings beyond the confines of her provincial life. But she tends to create a lot of interpersonal conflict while clinging to her fears as a way to protect herself from the deeper pain of separation that will surely accompany her declaration of independence.

Clarity results from the triumph of the need to know over the fear of knowing. We retain that sense of clear sight only when ready to receive the strength of the revealed vision. When mired in confusion, ask yourself: *Am I ready to know the truth? Am I ready to act on whatever knowledge wants to come through me?*

> *In an unbroken field, beyond the reach of ambition or avarice,*
> *ancient oaks stand heavy with drying summer foliage*
> *—their color flat and undistinguished.*
>
> *But when dawn wakes, casting her radiant eye*
> *on those mighty fellows, light*
> *touches leaf in stunning illumination,*
> *transforming dull brown to golden glory.*
> *(But so too are nearby shadows more pronounced.)*
>
> *Like the dawn, clarity illuminates,*
> *enhancing beauty—but may also reveal*
> *secrets that can no longer be kept.*

······˙··●

Can we cultivate moments of lucidity? Certainly breakthrough insights do not come in a vacuum, although their sudden appearance sometimes gives that impression.

Creative clarity has its roots in the felt-events of our lives—in a collection of life experiences stored in the body (whether consciously remembered or not). When creators immerse themselves in their subject matter—through play, exploration, practice, research, and study—this "in-gathering of memories," as the artist Philip Taaffe calls it, becomes the rich soil from which inspiration can spring. During creative work, a spontaneous insight results from a lifetime of living, learning, preparation, mastery of technique, and reflection.

A fine-furniture maker has this to say about persisting towards clarity, "When I was just starting out, I felt a deep attraction to the special character of fine woods, but didn't know how to bring it out. I spent a lot of time just learning the basics of my craft. I just went in totally blind, ruining things, starting again and again, but thinking and discovering new things all the time. It was very frustrating at times, but, after a while, it was like I could hear the wood speaking to me. But you have to have this experience of practice, frustration, and failure in order to really get clear about what you are doing."

······⋅·•

When actively working on a project, we sometimes need to step back in order to gain perspective. Sometimes clarity can only come with distance. Walk around the block, go to the movies, watch a sunset, take a hot bath, or perform some physical task such as filing papers, cleaning your desk, or washing the breakfast dishes. Relaxing the mind frequently stimulates the flow of insight.

At other times, persistence can energize a breakthrough. We must not give up at the first sign of difficulty—keep on working, even though it may feel like the work is going nowhere. Sometimes the only way out is through . . .

It feels like I've been typing pages and pages of drivel and superfluous ramblings. It's too stilted. There's no life here. My heart isn't in it. It's all cold cold cold. Interminable hours seem to pass and I haven't started having fun yet. I am convinced that I am failing. A small voice cries from the dark, "I can't do it, I just can't do it." Somehow, I keep on writing through the creeping edge of panic. I write whole paragraphs that continue to seem irrelevant.

Nothing works except that, even in my struggle, I focus intense attention on what I am doing. I sit back momentarily and sigh as I run my hands through my hair. My fingers snag in its coarse texture and I think that I might make better use of my time if I get up and wash it. I stare intently at the screen, absentmindedly twirling an unctuous tendril between my fingers.

Suddenly an opening occurs—everything seems fused with energy and unity as I start to see a way to bring the whole thing together. It's as if I'm standing both outside and inside the work simultaneously. A new urgency displaces any thoughts of personal hygiene. Shift a paragraph here, add a description there, and take this section out entirely. My body feels flooded with energy. And I write some more—only now I'm soaring!

······ · ·· ●

No matter what your creative medium, you can work for a long time, try every conceivable solution, and not find what you are looking for. Finally, you come to the point where you seem to have exhausted all possible directions. Just when you feel the most muddled, just when the inevitability of defeat calls like a siren's song—that's when conditions are ripe for an unexpected breakthrough.

The psychiatrist Carl Jung famously observed, "There is no light without shadow." Despite the difficulties, we need to permit ourselves to become lost—and perhaps suffer feelings of abandonment and hopelessness—before a way out reveals itself. Hidden within the murkiness of confusion and contradiction lies clarity. In her breathtaking invocation to the dark goddess Kali, poet May Sarton reminds us to value the mysterious forces that shape the creative spirit: "Help us to be always hopeful gardeners of the spirit, who know that without darkness nothing comes to birth and without light nothing flowers."

Further Reflections On Clarity

Clarity tells you what you need to know so you can take the next step in the creative process. If you wish to go deeper, explore one or more of the following questions. *Write, draw, dance, paint, meditate . . .*

☞ Am I ready to know the truth?

☞ Am I ready to release that which undermines my clarity?

☞ Once I achieve clarity, am I prepared to act on that knowledge?

☞ What scares me about stepping into my power? In what ways do I hide what I know from myself? From others?

☞ What is blocking my clarity? What is the payoff for remaining in uncertainty?

☞ What is right in front of me that I am unwilling to see? What would I create if I had clarity right now? What would I do or decide?

☞ What practices and habits best support my ability to tolerate the anxious uncertainty that precedes clarity?

☞ What else do I need to know before I can move forward?

. . . there comes a point where it just takes on a life of its own. There is a powerful force or energy and you are just riding it, serving it through your responses, actions.

—Source unknown

He couldn't remember sleeping or eating. The words simply poured out of him in a stream he could not control, nor question. . . .

—Brian Klugman

Engagement

I RELISH DAYS when I come to work inspired and ready to engage. On such occasions, my ideas can take shape with extraordinary rapidity. Engagement intimately connects the creator and the work through a give and take, a wordless dialogue, an exchange of energy that becomes so consuming we easily forget about everything else. Mundane concerns and responsibilities, even the need for sleep and food, dissipate in the urgency and excitement of passionate work. Although informed by a conscious purpose, the actual moment of engagement cannot be willed. *It is an act of surrender.* But surrender to what and to whom? We give ourselves to the creative current as it passes through us and also to the demands of the work. The greater our capacity to relinquish control, the more intense the creative encounter becomes.

A sculptor talks about the relationship between himself and his craft in this way: "I have an idea of what I am trying to do but the clay also wants to be something. I need to consider *its* wishes, not just my own. The process is all about me and the clay dancing together. Sometimes my hands lead and sometimes the clay leads. When everything is flowing, the feeling of harmony and well-being is just so tremendous—indescribable really—like a transfusion of energy."

······ · ··●

Engagement penetrates the surface veneer and sees into the mysterious heart of things. Constantin Brâncuşi, the patriarch of modern sculpture, was a passionate advocate of this sacred approach. True art needed to "draw out the essence of things," rather than reflect the distorted perceptions of the artist's ego or merely copy outward appearance. The creator's gaze should penetrate to the material's essence and discover a hidden soul awaiting liberation at the hands of the artist.

Such sensitivity, and the skill to bring the material to life, enables deep communion between the creator and his or her medium, whether painting, song, story, or even the abstraction of pure mathematics. Ask yourself: *How might increasing my own capacity for engagement enliven the experience of living, if only my own eyes can be persuaded to see—directly, freshly, deeply?*

······ · ··●

What actually happens during engagement? Little, if any, analytical dialogue occurs. Instead, we intuitively go with the flow; it is obvious what the next decision will be, we don't have to stop and think about it. Athletes refer to this state of total absorption as "playing in the zone"—a quality of consciousness that can be achieved once all physical, mental, and emotional resistance has dissolved. We become a *channel* through which words, brush strokes, musical notes, ideas, and actions flow seamlessly of their own accord. We feel we are giving birth to something organic rather than constructing something artificial.

An otherworldly quality pervades such moments because our usual sense of self-consciousness recedes into the background. An actor told me, "I'm not there anymore, I've become an antenna picking up signals that come to me through my body." During these times, the creative dance becomes its most complex, yet feels so utterly simple. "You let yourself invent moment to moment and see where it leads you, rather than planning and manipulating," says author and teacher Michele Cassou.

At the height of engagement, we frequently sift through various options without realizing we are making choices because it happens so effortlessly. The barriers we normally maintain between the inside of ourselves and the outside world dissolve into one simultaneous action—releasing a surge of unrestrained energy which carries us forward and beyond our usual limitations.

During the flow state, I am highly alert and functional, sometimes working on several parts of a project simultaneously, flipping through pages and pages of notes, going back and forth between chapters, while ideas and whole paragraphs sound themselves inside my mind. Somehow I am able to contain the complexity of all these competing suggestions and tasks while working calmly, executing each of them in turn. Yet in my normal waking state I am easily overwhelmed when I have too many things to do.

Whenever our thoughts, feelings, or actions interfere with the trance of work, we are no longer engaged. As my sculptor friend remarked, "As soon as I get too anxious or too analytical in an attempt to control everything, the dance ceases and the trance of working is broken."

·····················●

While the actual period of engagement feels like play or an exalted state, the process of *becoming* engaged may feel like drudgery. When we get ready to work, much of the labor involves getting out of our own way so that we can permit our creative juices to flow. A consultant-writer describes his pre-engagement experience squeamishly, "I can almost feel my skin crawling . . . it takes everything I have just to keep myself in the chair." As creators, we face conflicting emotions. On the one hand, anxious feelings urge us to flee; on the other hand, the work we long to do calls to us like the memory of a lover's embrace.

Successful creators resolve this duality through the judicious application of disciplined scheduling intermixed with appropriate flexibility and reward. As creators, we may spend several hours attempting to engage. Once achieved, preserving this productive yet fragile state of mind becomes paramount. Friends and family can sometimes find a creator's touchy behavior quite mysterious, even annoying, until they understand that the flow state needs to be protected and extended for as long as possible.

Years before I understood the delicacies of engagement, I called an artist-friend in order to retrieve something from her home. She specified the time I should come and when I tried to suggest an alternative, she was downright ornery. At the time, I remember wondering to myself, "What's the big deal?" I only want to drop by for a second and grab what I need. Aren't you going to be home all day anyway?"

I just didn't get it.

Now I understand that my friend wanted to welcome me when she could relax and fully enjoy my company. When she was engaged in passionate work, I would simply be an annoying intrusion. Her courage, maturity, and commitment allowed her to set clear boundaries—and risk alienating me—so that she could work undisturbed.

······ ·· ●

The vibrancy of creative energy can sometimes be an uncomfortable force. Energy may be, as William Blake wrote, "Eternal Delight," but for many of us, it is also "Eternal Terror." Out of fear, creators frequently resist the call to engagement. *Why do we avoid something that can feel so incredibly fantastic?*

We fear crossing the chasm between the two worlds of the mind: the ordinary, everyday perspective with its familiar reference points and constraints, and the realm of invention, which makes its own rules. During the crossing, we are neither here nor there—in a sense we are out of one mind but not yet into the other. That gap becomes an obstacle to engagement because of the discomfort of fear. A creative encounter invites us to enter a multidimensional world far broader and more ambiguous than our workaday world. The process of moving from the analytical mind to the creative mind sometimes triggers irrational emotional responses— many of which seem to be variations on losing control.

Bruce, an aspiring musician, struggles to stay connected to his work. "Whenever I start to get the feeling that things are happening, I get distracted—it's like I get into it and then I just can't sustain it." I ask Bruce to close his eyes and focus on the part of himself that refuses the connection to music. Bruce starts to laugh as he sees the teenage version of himself defiantly sitting in his room. "Ask him why he doesn't want to play," I suggest. Immediately, Bruce remembers how much he resented his parents for making him practice.

In the next moment, those past suffocating feelings of confinement and resentment over missing out on being with his friends flood Bruce's mind and body with surprising intensity. Even though he genuinely wants to play music, an old pattern—resistance to authority—keeps Bruce from being available to the possibilities in the present moment. Now that he can define the problem, Bruce can compromise with his inner adolescent's counterproductive strategy. *Acknowledging the legitimate need* behind his teenage disruptive behavior, Bruce schedules time for recreation immediately following practice sessions. He also stops pushing himself so relentlessly. Bruce's teenage self feels seen and respected—he's part of a team now, rather than a maladjusted rebel. The tools of self-awareness and internal negotiation empower Bruce to remain engaged with his music while healing and integrating valuable aspects of his inner life.

······ˑ··●

As we mature in our relationship to creative uncertainty and the demands of engagement, we will discover great pleasure in the spontaneous interplay between ourselves and this intangible something that is in the process of becoming. At its peak, engagement feels like a fusion of our bodies with whatever we are working on; our creations become part of us as we become part of them. Wholehearted engagement borders on devotion—a kind of love affair with the Muse herself. In permitting ourselves to be transported into and under the skin of our creations, we open ourselves to hidden realms of meaning. And when we encounter those depths—and then infuse our creations with what we meet there—grace intertwines with rapture.

Further Reflections On Engagement

How easily can you suspend judgmental thinking in order to engage the flow of creative inspiration? If you wish to go deeper, explore one or more of the following questions. *Write, draw, dance, paint, meditate . . .*

☞ In what activities do I find myself losing track of time?

☞ What is my relationship to the creative flow: Do I allow it to guide me or do I force it to my will?

☞ In what ways does my working environment either help or hinder my capacity to engage? How much structure, control, chaos, safety, conflict, harmony, support, quiet, privacy, or pressure do I need to achieve engagement?

☞ Do I value and protect my time for creative work? Where do I sometimes say yes to please others and then later regret it? What price do I pay? What boundaries do I need to set with the people I love?

☞ Is the prospect of disappearing into the intensity of my passions scary or exciting or both?

☞ Consider Cézanne: "A day is coming when a carrot, freshly observed, will set off a revolution." How might this idea revolutionize my view of myself and the outside world?

What you respond to in any work of art is the artist's struggle against his or her own limitations.

—Saul Steinberg

Every creator painfully experiences the chasm between his inner vision and its ultimate execution.

—Isaac Singer

Only if the tension between anxiety and fascination is held, will the combustion point occur.

—Marion Woodman

Tension

AS CREATORS, WE LIVE our working lives at the edge, wandering the outskirts of our most private vulnerabilities. The strain of pushing the edges of our personal boundaries energizes and moves our creative work toward authenticity. During the creative process, sources of tension proliferate and can inspire serious anxiety. Eventually, if we are to make any progress, if we hope to complete a work of any depth, we must come to accept stress, uncertainty, and insecurity as companions on the journey.

A woman returns on a full scholarship to graduate school after a twenty-year absence from the world of academia. Although ecstatic over the opportunity, she battles anxieties about whether she is too old. A successful businessman wants to invest in a low-income housing project. Suffering sleepless nights, he wonders whether or not to proceed with this worthy but risky venture. A playwright-director has been invited to present a new work at a local theater. In the midst of rehearsals, she suddenly feels overwhelmed with doubts about whether she can pull it off.

One question usually resounds the loudest during the course of any new adventure, *"Do I have what it takes to do it?"* This query, perhaps more than any other, prevents most people from ever taking the first step and continues to reassert its challenge, even after we have been working for years. The confoundedly maddening answer is almost always, "yes and no."

The tension resides in this bittersweet recognition: We will almost always fail to produce something that exactly matches the original inspiration. A poignant fact of creation is that what we dream, what we desire, inevitably exceeds our imperfect execution, and the gap between conception and the limitations of manifestation violates our longing for perfection. Still, we must proceed. We must recognize the worthiness of making an effort, finding value and meaning in the results. We must or we will drive ourselves crazy. So what we do is strive. We strive in the face of insufferable knowledge that, at one level, we will surely fail—all the while making sure that we do not fail ourselves, that we do not sell ourselves short.

Holding that edge takes a lot of strength. But if we can hold it, we discover something infinitely interesting and satisfying. The labor of bringing the work into being necessitates a negotiation between the interior landscape of our ideals and the practical limitations of our skills in the real world. This negotiation, this dialogue of examination and discovery, this struggle to realize something, makes the whole project worthwhile.

The returning student may not get straight A's every semester, the businessman may not make as large a financial return as he would have if he had invested in a fast-growth technology company, and the director may not get a standing ovation for her new play. But each of them will succeed in some way they cannot predict or outwardly measure. By stretching themselves within the tension of doubt, each of them can experience fulfillment in a fidelity of purpose that will inspire other acts of creative risk.

······‥‥●

Another source of creative tension occurs when we have a substantial amount of the work completed, but still can't see the finish line. Somewhere along the way, the project seems to overrun its boundaries and mushroom out in all directions.

During this period, I sometimes wake up to the strange sensation of a soft, doughy thing covering my face. One night I find myself gasping for air, certain I am dying of suffocation. Frankly, I had always been too embarrassed to admit that I was haunted by an oversized version of the Pillsbury Doughboy. But, the other day, I heard a city planner describe a surprisingly similar feeling. "Whenever I get to the phase of a project where I don't have control, it's like I'm trapped under a giant water balloon. I try and try to push it off of me, but no matter where I push, another part oozes over and I can't get any leverage. It's like I am totally helpless."

The farther along we get into the work, the harder it seems to control. The resulting state of flux frequently ushers in a vigorous internal struggle (a kind of tension) between what we consciously have in mind and that *unknown other* that is struggling to be born.

Certain phases of a project have an expected linearity. After I've done my musing, thinking, and research, I usually have some idea about where I am headed. With the starting point in clear sight, I plunge ahead in eager urgency. For a while, I think I know exactly where the next step is, and the next. Such certainty, however temporary, empowers and energizes—while it lasts.

At some point, the process gradually becomes more circular and complex—rather than just *giving* direction, I am also *taking* it as well. The piece takes on a life of its own, and our relationship feels infused with well-being and harmony—at least for a while. A balance exists between what I want to do and what the piece wants me to do. Our connection feels seamless.

Then the balance of power shifts. The work grows bigger and bigger as I shrink progressively smaller. The honeymoon ends and we move into the power struggle phase. I can never quite sense exactly when the shift will happen; there must be signs but I don't take any notice of them while entranced in my romantic bliss. But one day, I walk into the studio and this warm, beautiful creation now seems cold, hard, and ugly. I react with dismay: "You're not what I expected; I thought you were one thing but you are really something else." As if to confirm the obvious, the *creature* now rears up and looms large, threatening to crush me with its immense unwieldiness. Panic urges me to run for a high and clear place before the creature pulls me into a vast netherworld.

If this relationship is going to succeed, I must regain some semblance of control—not too much, mind you, but enough so that I won't become paralyzed. So after a trip to the kitchen for a slice of pie—a girl's got to keep her energy up—I throw back my shoulders and stride back toward the beast, who by this time is mighty angry.

······'··●

Somewhere in the life of your project, you will make an ogre of the very thing that you love and so carefully nurture—most likely because it demands so much from you. The project you love will always ask more than you anticipated. Naturally, this challenge turns out to be something that you feel reluctant to do—think about the situation in a new way, probe some dark and forgotten corner of your psyche that you'd just as soon ignore, or redo six months of work in light of a fatal flaw. *Can you find the willingness, stamina, and discipline to give even more than you bargained for?*

Making, doing, or becoming something new is alternately exciting, miraculous, and difficult. The love-hate relationship you inevitably feel toward your work fires the creative juices, making your relationship to the work stronger, provided you don't allow negative feelings to gain the upper hand. Look the creature straight in the eye, wait, contemplate, and if nothing is forthcoming, take a break and come back again later. Do this over and over until a sudden understanding between you and the beast moves the work forward, relieving the tension.

Creators bring to life something silent and unseen—an idea, a feeling, a mystery—and coax it to speak out in tangible recognition. As the demands of our work stretch us to our limits, the energy and intensity can become so fierce that we aren't certain whether we'll survive it. Engaging this dynamic process opens us, sometimes painfully and against our will, to a wider field of experience and perception— ultimately spurring further growth. To dare risk, to bear uncertainty, to endure tension—these are the elements of the creative process that strengthen the human spirit.

Further Reflections on Tension

The *right* level of tension stimulates creative thinking and peak performance. If you wish to go deeper, explore one or more of the following questions. *Write, draw, dance, paint, meditate . . .*

☞ Where does my vision exceed my current reality? How can I hold the *creative* tension between these two points, as I work toward a resolution?

☞ In what ways do I increase *negative* tension? (Beating myself up? Dwelling on mistakes? Complaining?)

☞ What sensations do I experience in my body when the results of my efforts differ significantly from my original vision? (Am I anxious, excited, frustrated, or something else?)

☞ Are failures and obstacles an important part of my process or impediments to achieving my goals?

☞ Do I avoid the moment of creative encounter because I don't want to feel the tension inherent in the process? Where have I settled for less in order to relieve the discomfort of creative tension?

☞ When the intensity of creative tension triggers feelings of distress and discouragement, how can I find ease? What small step can I take? What people, practices, and activities help me detach, relax, and play so I can return to my work ready to engage? Hint: Take one minute to *focus* on your breath, *rest* your mind, and *ground* your body in the present moment.

☞ Consider David Whyte: "What disturbs and then nourishes has everything we need . . ."

The most important tool the artist fashions through
constant practice is faith in his ability to produce
miracles when they are needed.

—Mark Rothko

When Pablo Casals reached ninety-five, a young
reporter asked him a question: "Mr. Casals, you are
ninety-five and the greatest cellist who ever lived. Why
do you still practice six hours a day?" Casals answered,
"Because I think I'm finally making progress."

—Source unknown

Consistency

CREATORS DELIGHT IN the ease of engagement, when every intuition holds a world of possibilities, when creativity flows as naturally as breathing. At such times, we can't wait to get to work. But when inspiration evaporates, the last place we want to be is in our offices or studios. We need the structure of consistent work habits, or we will likely give up once the period of effortless flow abates.

A businessman who runs marathons spoke to me about the necessity of meeting inspiration halfway, not waiting for it to find him. "If I wait for the mood to strike I can easily become lethargic and unresponsive. I know that motivation will come if I just get out there and put one foot in front of the other. There are guys out there who are much younger and possess more spontaneous energy than I do, but they throw in the towel at the least difficulty. That is why, in spite of a natural advantage, they accomplish so little, and what they do accomplish is rather inconsistent."

No matter the passion—running, painting, or parenting—creators need to balance occasions of inspired serendipity with the discipline of consistent practice and repetitive routine. Showing up to work consistently helps to ground those flights of imaginative fancy and hone the technique that turns those untamed fancies into a form of communication that others can recognize and receive. The most incisive insights will never be communicated if they can't be captured in craft. Practice enables discovery and gradual mastery. The most talented composer of prose who lacks the ability to sit and actually write—hour after hour, day after day—turns all that talent into nothing but bits of flotsam in a vast sea.

······˙··●

Conscientious work habits protect our capacity to work productively because consistency *regulates* energy. The structure of routine provides a stable foundation, steadying us against the destabilizing effects of chaos and impulse. Here's what happens when I give in to impulse . . .

I wake up uncharacteristically early and wander into my office. I turn on the computer thinking I will check my email and then move on to the activities I have planned for the day—which do not include writing. But I can't resist sneaking a peek at yesterday's efforts. "I'll just read it through once," I tell myself . . . The next time I look up, it is five o'clock in the afternoon—almost eleven hours have passed unnoticed—and here I sit, still in my bathrobe. I suddenly realize that although the day has been productive from the standpoint of creative work, I haven't taken a shower or eaten a morsel, not to mention grocery shopping or those bills glaring at me from the corner of my desk. The day has slipped away from me.

Every so often, capricious bursts of work can help move a project forward, but too many of these bursts in a row shreds the routine of daily life, damaging a creator's relationships, finances, and health. Ask yourself: *What adjustments might I make to prevent my creative work from devouring me body and soul?*

······ ·· ●

Consistent practice also *generates* energy. Regular work routines give us a reason to keep going during those periods when we feel flat and uninspired. "It's about knowing how to work," says award-winning author Ann Patchett. "Sometimes the process is very far away from inspiration. You need to sit down and do it."

My client, an aspiring painter, has stopped going to his studio. "All I feel is bored and empty; nothing happens." I encourage him to keep going anyway, to establish a rhythm of time and accountability so that he might learn to trust his capacity to work under all circumstances. "Paint from the emptiness, let the emptiness show you something." After a few weeks of "painting *sludge*," as he calls it, he reports an increase in confidence, concentration, and the emergence of "an interesting new direction."

At times, we need a break from the routine of working. But more often than not, the project in progress requires the structure of consistent work habits to reenergize and focus inspiration.

······ ·· ●

There's no getting around it. If you want to make progress, if you desire to create something of substance, if you want to grow and deepen within yourself and your craft, you need to practice, practice, practice.

I have learned the hard way about the rewards of practice and the high costs of inconsistency. One of my greatest regrets is giving up the piano. I studied for several years as a child but my commitment to practice was always superficial and haphazard at best. Still, I was able to slide by and was a promising student in spite of myself. I remember feeling the music whole and complete inside my body and I wanted to play it that same way, but technique was not something that came as effortlessly as artistry. Easily bored with routine, I lacked the discipline to work consistently at developing the technical skills that would have coaxed the music from my body. As the requirements of the music began to outstrip my ability to fake it, something had to give.

On Thursday afternoon my piano teacher, Mrs. Guttentag, comes to the door and presses the bell. I stand behind the door, listening to the sounding of the chimes until their faint reverberation announces that my obstinacy has finally won the day.

Although I had freed myself from the monotony of practice, my victory carried hidden costs that would haunt me for years to come. A pattern of starting and stopping would continue well into adulthood. It was always the same. At first, I blasted off like a rocket—propelled by my initial enthusiasm and natural talent. But after a period of time, I stopped steadily climbing. I felt myself drifting off course, becoming frustrated or even, heaven forbid, sliding backward. Lacking a blueprint for the process, I failed to endure.

Eventually, I realized that when advancement stops, or even retreats, we have arrived at a critical place in the process. Here, adrift in outer and inner space, we find true meaning within our work. Consistent work habits become the mothership, sustaining us despite any signs of outward progress until we learn what we need to learn, discover what we need to discover—igniting the second-stage booster which propels us to the next level.

Natural ability gets us only so far. If we listen to what great athletes and creators say about their success, we hear repeatedly that hard work and consistent effort count much more than raw talent. To paraphrase Thomas Edison, *creativity* is one percent inspiration and ninety-nine percent perspiration. If we don't take our desires seriously enough, we can't progress beyond the dabbling stage. We begin over and over again, never getting far, never learning how to work steadfastly through boredom, chaos, anxiety, elation, frustration, fatigue, triumph—never discovering the deeper rewards of consistency.

······•

We can't depend on work progressing smoothly day after day. Still, we must continue. We must develop some pattern of consistency that supports the attainment of something beyond a series of fragmented, disconnected encounters. But routines only succeed when we feel nourished by them. *They must meet us where we are in our process in order to take us where we'd like to be.*

My client Gary wants to get back into shape after years of sedentary living. A year ago, he consulted a doctor who put him on a low-fat diet and thirty minutes of aerobic exercise three times a week. The doctor's plan certainly sounded reasonable enough—in theory. But once Gary put the plan into practice, he experienced it as "an exhausting regime of deprivation." After weeks and weeks of pushing himself to comply, Gary started to falter and after a period of faltering, he gave up completely.

I sense that Gary sincerely wants a healthier lifestyle, otherwise he would not have made an appointment with me to find out what went wrong. "Even though you have a strong desire to make this change," I explain, "you defeated yourself by trying to accomplish too much too soon, and by failing to assert yourself during the initial consultation with your doctor."

During our visit, I ask him to consider looking at his relapse with a creative attitude. "It doesn't require any original thought to follow someone else's plan for you. Why not accept your failure to conform to the requirements of this particular program and redesign it to suit your own needs?"

Gary makes the difficult decision to scale back his ambitions considerably. He excludes only those foods he can easily give up and agrees to walk for fifteen minutes once a week. This plan is drastically inadequate when compared to the ideal, but he admits with considerable embarrassment, "This is all I am capable of."

"For the moment," I remind him. "This is only a place to start; it's not the end."

Indeed, within six months Gary finds himself walking for longer periods of time, refusing many of his fatty favorites more often, and growing confident enough to add another fifteen minute walk to the schedule. *By supporting himself in making small efforts, Gary stimulates his natural desire to do more.*

Consistency should not suffocate the spirit, but liberate it. Many of us attempt routines that are out of sync with our most basic needs—and consequently fail. We end up blindly following the recommendations of friends, experts, and teachers instead of integrating their often sound advice with the requirements of our unique temperaments, limitations, and lifestyles. Even the best advice falls short if we can't make it work. We need to respect our idiosyncratic tendencies and permit them to inform not only our work, but the manner in which we accomplish it.

······ ··•

When we do something consistently, it becomes the center of our lives, bringing us into profound relationship with ourselves. Consistency with time becomes a meditation. Everything that we are and everything we are not confronts us each time we show up. That's one big reason why we resist the routine of creative work. As soon as we work with any regularity at all, the situation becomes a mirror reflecting back to us whatever we bring to the process.

The rhythm of practice takes us inside ourselves. A sensation . . . a fragment of memory . . . a broken heart can mingle alongside an unspoken ambition or a brilliant idea. When we willingly meet ourselves again and again, a deep and abiding trust forms in the center of our being. And from this stable core grows a powerful groundswell of energy, competence, and confidence that readies us for future and greater accomplishment. As creators, we must do things over and over and over until the muse speaks to us, until she reaches out and infuses us with inspiration.

Further Reflections on Consistency

Reaping the rewards of consistency requires time, discipline, and nonattachment to results. If you wish to go deeper, explore one or more of the following questions. *Write, draw, dance, paint, meditate . . .*

☞ What is the optimal time and place for me to be productive?

☞ How long does it actually take me to make meaningful progress on an important project? Do I give myself enough time to work on this one thing? (Be careful here; we tend to overestimate what we can do in a short period, and underestimate what we can do over a long period.)

☞ Do I give myself the best chance for sticking with what matters most, or do I chop up the day into bits and pieces, undermining my creative work with scheduling conflicts?

☞ What encourages me to keep working? What gets in the way? What structures, habits, practices, rituals, and rewards can I put in place to support creative consistency?

☞ Consider Henry Miller: "To paint is the thing. To paint each day. Not to turn out masterpieces . . ."

To do great work a man must be very idle
as well as very industrious.

—Samuel Butler

. . . it's been decided that if you lie down
no one will die.

—Robert Bly

I always forget how important the empty days are,
how important it may be sometimes not to expect to
produce anything, even a few lines in a journal.

—May Sarton

Rest

PASSIONATE WORK PLACES enormous energy demands on our bodies
and psyches, sometimes for inordinate amounts of time. The experience of creating can be exhilarating, but also agitating and exhausting.
While we work fully engaged in the imaginal world, we can easily
lose touch with the reality of our human needs. We demand more and
more from our bodies. We expect them to keep on going; to keep on
supplying us with the energy we need to work, without stopping to
replenish the source of that energy. If we aren't careful, we can push
ourselves to the point where we start hating the work because it drains
us, rather than providing nourishment. We need to eat, we need to
sleep, we need companionship, we need to exercise our bodies. And
from time to time, we need to rest.

Simply rest.

When we push the limits of our capacity, adequate rest deepens, inspires, and moves the work forward. When we let go of activity, we shift into a place where we can digest and reflect. Creators need to do more than move mechanically through their experience; they must take time to extract the juice from a particular encounter, squeezing the fruit of experience down to its essence and distilling some vital or compelling truth that finds its ultimate expression in the work.

My actor friend Adam rehearses a new play. His character suffers from delusions that he is the Holy Roman Emperor. When I ask Adam how the matter of rest relates to his work, he has quite a lot of interesting things to say on the subject.

"This is one of the most demanding roles I have ever played. During rehearsal the director asks for a lot of things I can't do right then because I don't have an internal understanding of what he wants. I can only hear him describing something to me. I can't find it in myself yet, except very mechanically. It is particularly exhausting when I am trying to do something that is just beyond my reach."

How do you cope with feeling so overwhelmed?

"To keep working on the problem when I'm really tired is unproductive. I need to go home, unwind, and put aside the character. I actually have to ground myself and visualize the character's energy running out of me, the connection is that intense. Then I listen to music, something that puts me in a really different space. After a good night's rest, I'm ready to experiment and search and find an answer within myself to what the director is looking for."

So resting opens a space to solve the dilemma?

"Definitely. To understand the character from my own experience I have to really grasp what it means to be deluded. I begin to contemplate the times I've deluded myself—like when I've imagined that a relationship is possible with someone where it would be obvious to any outsider that it isn't. And during that reflection, I think about my own neediness; I experience the truth about obsession, not what it is so much, as where it comes from. It is only then that I realize how to do what the director is asking."

When we alternate periods of intense engagement with periods of rest, we honor the natural rhythm of the creative process: the body relaxes from the tension of working; the mind opens and softens; insight bubbles up from the underground spring; and we return to work infused with energy, ideas, and new understanding.

······ ·· ●

But we don't rest simply to do more work. In rest, we release the mind, restore the body, and rejuvenate the spirit. When we rest, we wander without ambition, losing ourselves in the lushness of a rich green, in the quiet murmur of a languid stream, in the imperceptible drift of clouds, in the timeless themes of a captivating novel. In the uneventful passing of the days, we gather together those pieces of ourselves that had become scattered and forgotten in the debris of a busy life. We discover ourselves anew.

In my forties, I find myself entering a period of ambivalence. I spent the preceding years building a life that was energized, focused, and filled with involvements that really meant something to me. Now, I feel this sense of purpose being displaced by a creeping restlessness. I want to go somewhere. Anywhere. I feel a desperate need to get away from everything that is familiar. Yet at the same time, it seems like too much work to leave. This contradiction mystifies me, although my journal entry from the time certainly sounds clear enough: "I just want to rest . . . to ramble, aimless . . . experience without demand. Incubate, receive, heal. Rest my spirit."

How many ways can I say it? I read the words but underestimate their significance. After taking several weeks of vacation, I plunge back into my life, redoubling my efforts. I have two shows to prepare, clients to see, galleries to query, columns to write, a publication to produce, and a social life to maintain. I simply cannot slow down long enough to absorb the truth . . . that my life as I know it is no longer sustainable.

It takes another year before my malaise grinds down my body. Unable to concentrate or gather strength for more than the most basic tasks, I finally come to a frightening realization—I am on the verge of collapse. Finally, I am forced to admit that the life that I have worked so hard to create—the life that contains so much of what matters most to me, the life that defines me professionally, personally, and creatively— can no longer support me. The pace, the discipline, and the organization required to maintain it all has exhausted my spirit at a profound level. I need to stop. I need to rest.

Although I initially fight the change with every fiber of my being, it turns out to be—as is often the case with situations we violently resist—one of the best things that could have happened. Once I acknowledge the seriousness of the situation, I resolve to do whatever is necessary to regenerate my spirit.

I make the decision to embark on a period of *radical rest*.

······ · ··●

I put aside most of the trappings and involvements of my current life—without any expectation that I will embrace them again—and retreat from the world. My boyfriend and I rent a secluded house surrounded by forty acres of forested land and live a simple life that centers on the basics I had no time for until now—cooking, gardening, napping, puttering, reading novels, raising animals. I see a few clients, but have neither the energy nor the desire to write or paint.

I struggle to adjust to the slower pace. But after a while, I begin to connect with the ancient and enduring current that flows beneath the frantic pace of modern life. I find myself moving with the natural rhythms of my body and less in accordance with a list of things that demand doing. For the first time in a long time, I stop forcing things— nothing matters so much that it can't be put off until tomorrow. I develop a whole new relationship with time because I have so much more of it than before. I express my creativity through a variety of home-centered activities, but I also spend many days sitting and looking out at vistas of sky and pine and chaparral, not moving for long periods of time. Sometimes I forget what day it is.

In repose, I find myself becoming softer and more present, but rest is not always so peaceful. Anxiety, depression, and grief move into the foreground when I can no longer count on familiar competencies to stand between me and my vulnerability. Stormy days—where I feel myself to be awash in self-doubt and regret for past mistakes, or in fear of an unknown destiny—melt into days that seem endlessly glorious and satisfying. In permitting all these feelings (and the memories that accompany them) to be part of my experience, I release a reservoir of stagnant emotional energy that had taken up space in my cells, muscles, organs, and psyche. Slowly, I feel myself healing.

Immersing myself in the silent majesty of the natural world, while emptying out everything that has previously filled me, makes room for something new and unexpected. After nearly two years, the Universe begins to summon me. An invitation to write for an online magazine, an appearance on a PBS television series, and the inspiration and strength to begin this book were all gifts that came, one after the other, like the bounty of a summer harvest.

When we rest, we give ourselves the most precious gift of all—the gift of time. Time to think, time to be, time to putter without the demand that we accomplish something constructive. We need not feel alarmed when we have intervals where we don't achieve anything significant, when we fail to push ourselves to the absolute limit. Like the farmer's fields lying fallow under a blanket of snow, the creative response needs to replenish itself. Rest allows us to rebuild vital nutrients that nourish the creative soil.

Further Reflections On Rest

Is fatigue zapping your creative juices? If you wish to go deeper, explore one or more of the following questions. *Write, draw, dance, paint, meditate . . .*

➥ How much rest do I need to replenish my creative juices?

➥ How does fatigue impact the quality of my creative work? When is the optimal time for me to take a break from work?

➥ What would happen if rest was as important to me as work? Could unplugging for periods of time actually help me accomplish more?

➥ Do I hide my real need for downtime because I'm afraid of being judged as lazy? Or do I stay busy to avoid the thoughts and feelings that surface once I stop and rest?

➥ Even if I can't embark on a period of *radical rest*, how might I create shorter respites for creative renewal and restoration?

➥ What brings me a feeling of being rested and recharged? (Do any of these restful options sound inviting—going to the movies or an art show, watching a live performance, taking a workshop just for fun, power napping, getting out into nature, talking with a friend, soaking in a tub, meditating, reading a mystery, or doing absolutely nothing?)

Take refuge in your senses, open up to all the small
miracles you rushed through.

— *John O'Donohue*

It's as hard to get from almost finished to finished
as to get from beginning to almost done.

—Elinor Fuchs

With completion, we understand bravery and desire
and the fact that these two things must always remain
hand in glove.

—Whitney Otto

Whatever it takes to finish things, finish. You will
learn more from a glorious failure than you ever will
from something you never finished.

—Neil Gaiman

6
Finishing

A S WE PROGRESS TOWARD the culmination of our efforts, we finally glimpse sight of the goal. Some creators have a natural tendency to finish what they start, while others indulge in all manner of distractions to avoid the fatal moment, the ultimate conclusion. As one of my readers wrote, "I get to page 245 in my novel—one scene from the end, and suddenly start living at Target. There is so much underwear I absolutely have to buy. So much more I have to launder, fold, and reorganize in drawers at home."

Often we delay completion because we dread the moment of judgment that must come once we stop, survey our efforts, and ask ourselves the tough, but essential question: *Have I done what I set out to do?*

When we embark on a creative journey, we travel toward a destination of unknown dimensions. Imagination, courage, and perseverance generate solutions to numerous dilemmas we encounter along the way. But how do we know we have arrived?

Sometimes we think we have arrived, but it turns out to be just another threshold, another portal to further discovery. Ask yourself: *Am I holding something in reserve? Do I sense something missing?* Then, by all means, keep going if it brings you closer to your truth. But do not let needling anxiety keep you from recognizing your destination.

When we become too anxious, we may go too far, and revise the life out of our inspirations. In trying to perfect the imperfectible, we only succeed in draining our creations of their potency. If something can be tested and proven objectively, so much the better. However, in the arts, completion tends to be subjective—the ultimate test we must pass is our own.

Experienced creators intuitively sense when all the strands of a project come together. Completion may announce itself as a subtle but innate recognition, an inexplicable feeling of the familiar, or a felt-sensation that can sometimes be described as "coming home." In the absence of objective, verifiable criteria for completion, creators must rely on their senses. "It's done when it *tastes* done," says the poet Gary Snyder. In lieu of a quantifiable measurement, our destination will *feel real* once we have arrived.

Completion makes our desire fully real. As the embodiment of our vision stands before us, we resonate with the timeless, soul-satisfying pleasure of having made something. And, perhaps, a quiet sense of honor for a promise kept.

Qualities that help us cross the finish line include *integrity*, *judgment*, *compromise*, *fulfillment*, and *emptiness*.

Integrity keeps us true to our own voice. *Judgment* applies critical thinking skills to evaluate and polish the work. *Compromise* transforms conflicts into improvements that strengthen the final product or ready it for the marketplace. *Fulfillment* rewards us with the satisfaction of having done what we set out to do. *Emptiness* provides a quiet space for reflection that prepares us to let go of the current project before moving on to the next.

Every artist dips his brush in his own soul,
and paints his own nature into his pictures.

—Henry Ward Beecher

You have to do what you do and love what you are
doing, and hopefully, other people will like it too.

—Carol Burnett

It is by remaining faithful to the contingencies
and peculiarities of your own experience and the
vagaries of your own nature that you stand the
greatest chance of conveying something.

—Geoff Dyer

Integrity

CREATORS WITH INTEGRITY have the capacity to complete work of substance—not necessarily perfect work, not necessarily work that garners fame and fortune, but work that speaks to something worthwhile. Unless you fully invest your efforts with the truth of your feelings and perceptions, the final product will lack energy, falling short of conveying a convincing perspective.

I often work with creators who fail to express a distinctive vision. Although Michael has no problem finishing work, he finds the whole process dispiriting. Looking at his portfolio, I see the reason for his waning enthusiasm: His technically accomplished paintings please the eye, but lack a soul. Something crucial is missing—the artist. It's as if no one is home.

Gloria studies for her MFA and worries about finding a niche within established artistic tradition. She knows how to get started on an idea, but fails to complete any work beyond what her instructors assign. When attempting to pursue her own projects, Gloria's creative focus becomes sidetracked by incessant mental comparisons between her work and the masterpieces in her field. By putting so much attention outside of her own process, Gloria feels too intimidated to trust her own vision.

In both cases, these creators fear placing themselves and their convictions at the center of their process. Consequently, their work lacks integrity—it lacks an authentic expression of personal truth.

The strongest work—work that communicates a palpable spirit—comes from creators who follow their own truth. Obviously, something that feels empty and meaningless to you will certainly fail to move anyone else. So you not only need a vision, you also need the inner strength to express the truth of that vision. Ask yourself: *What feels creatively compelling to me?* Whatever your truth, explore it, deeply, thoroughly. You will most likely discover that it matters to others as well.

······'··●

Maintaining integrity of vision from start to finish requires a strong sense of self, one that does not follow the crowd or give way in order to appease others. Instead, seek to uncover and express your own unique nature. *Where do I discover such an authentic self?* Start by exploring the experiences that have made you who you are.

Authentic creative expression begins when you become aware of the tremendous wealth of resources contained within you—and then learn to trust them, and to count on them. Such vital knowledge makes it possible to risk and fail, to face all manner of difficulty, yet know that you possess a quality of character or a particular talent that will eventually help you prevail.

Much of our potential comes to us through our family and the legacy of our ancestors. We lose our best and most important resources when we fail to come to terms with our past. Clients who complain about being uncreative frequently discount their personal history, judging it as uninteresting or too ordinary to hold any creative promise.

Others reject or rebel against their families of origin with an intensity that freezes them in early experiences of negativity and pain. When we get stuck recycling the past or reacting against it, we cannot claim the gifts that are hidden in the debris of even the most difficult upbringing. Tucked away, in what appear to be barren places, lie keys to a unique identity and authentic nuggets of character.

I consider myself a late bloomer, creatively speaking, in part because the stories I told myself about my mother's limitations kept hurt and anger alive, sapping my creative energy. I defined myself by my past—specifically, my mother's inability to care for me. To make matters more difficult, my childhood strategy for coping with my inability to change the situation was to blame HER. I clung to the certainty that there was actually something she could do. I told myself she was simply too weak or worse, she didn't love me enough to change. (In matters of the heart, we often find it hard to tell the difference between *what is true in fact* and what feels emotionally true.)

Although my mother had not been a daily presence in my life since the age of ten, my responses to adversity continued to be defined by the contours of her absence. The long-practiced habit of placing responsibility outside myself had taken root deep inside my psyche, damaging my sense of power and integrity. Over the years, my personal truth—my story, my identity—became so focused on *deficit* that I was unable to claim anything of value from the most significant relationship in my life. In casting my mother out, I demonized part of my own soul. My single-minded perception of my mother's shortcomings resulted in my shortchanging myself: *If she was lacking, then so am I; if she gave me nothing, then I have nothing; if I have nothing, then I am nothing.* Even though I could be an enthusiastic starter, I allowed a narrative of abandonment, blame, and deficiency to hold me back—I struggled to find the inner resources I needed to acknowledge, let alone finish, anything that truly mattered to me.

······ꞏꞏ●

We often assume our early understanding about the meaning of our experience will serve us for a lifetime. But what feels true at one stage of life becomes a lie at another. Once upon a time, the comforting certainty of my old story gave me a kind of perverse strength, helping me survive. Now, believing myself to be somehow deficient as a result of my mother's actions was making my life tougher than it needed to be. I needed a new story—one that told a more complete truth—or I would cease growing creatively.

I had to set myself free.

To unburden my authentic self, I needed to crack open the wall of resentment that surrounded and protected me from my pain. I needed to move beyond my childhood understanding and discover more about who I was, who my mother was, and the reality we shared. Authenticity can only be uncovered by pushing beyond boundaries. Uncovering and transforming outmoded patterns of thinking meant mining my past for buried treasure—and recovering those missing nuggets, the ones I needed in order to restore my creative integrity.

With the help of a talented therapist, what I found was so simple and so obvious I couldn't believe I hadn't seen it before. In the midst of all the devastation, I somehow received much more than my heartbreak allowed me to remember: I discovered my mother's empathy, her gentleness, and her spontaneous laughter.

During one session, I finally move beyond the seemingly endless round of sad stories. . .

I feel a sharp tear as my heart breaks open. Tears of forgotten happiness begin streaming down my face. It is the first tangible memory of my mother's creative vitality unencumbered by depression . . . I am very young. My mother and I are laughing in the kitchen. We are decorating a cake while belting out the lyrics to our favorite song, "Side By Side." I pour a big glob of food coloring into the frosting, turning it a hideous shade of dark green. But she just sings louder, letting the lyrics carry us through the culinary disaster . . . "Just as long as we're together, it really doesn't matter at all."

It had once been too difficult for me to hold such fleeting moments of happiness alongside the painful reality of daily disappointment. Now, it didn't matter how fleeting it was; what mattered was how these new truths enlarged my vision of my mother. During subsequent sessions, I recall the many hours she spent reading to me in her bed when she could do little else. I lost her to that bed she rarely left, but she also gifted me her curiosity, and her love of knowledge for its own sake. At the time, it didn't seem like enough, but that single grace ended up saving my life.

I have experienced no greater pain than feeling the truth of being loved when love falls short. But what I received in exchange for facing the truth made it worthwhile. I have a new, more complete story about my mother's love for me and mine for her. We both missed out because of her ineffable sorrow, but I can finally take comfort in her love, all these years later. In restoring my mother's fullness, I recovered my own.

······•

The human spirit is incredibly resilient. *Your spirit is incredibly resilient.* And it has gone to great lengths to preserve itself, hoping that one day you will take the time to search through the rubble and restore the luster. We can make the *journey home* to complete ourselves; or, no matter what we finish, our creations will never feel complete.

Even though many of us have stories we wouldn't have chosen, we need to find a way to embrace them anyway. We can never completely escape who we are and where we come from, but we can transform our experience by probing and using it. The more you dare to delve into the experiences of your life, the more authentic you become. And, the more authentic you become, the more unique and powerful your work becomes. You *can* complete something vibrant and honest if you channel the force of your convictions.

Further Reflections On Integrity

What is your truth? If you wish to go deeper, explore one or more of the following questions. *Write, draw, dance, paint, meditate . . .*

☞ The artist Robert Rauschenberg once said, "Anything you do will be an abuse of somebody else's aesthetics." Which is more important to me: fitting in or finding and expressing my authentic voice?

☞ How much outside approval do I need to feel validated as a creator? Under what circumstances do I feel pressured to conform?

☞ To what degree do my decisions and actions align with my values? What helps me take care of my authentic self?

☞ How can I organize my life around the priorities that matter most to me?

☞ In what ways do I deceive myself and others? What am I attempting to hide?

☞ What limiting self-concepts do my old stories perpetuate? How does that impact my ability to create authentic work? Is there a truer reality pulsing beneath an old story I keep telling and retelling?

☞ Am I in flight from my past? What is unfinished in my life? Will I feel differently about myself when I do complete it?

☞ Am I creating for myself or the approval of others? Is it more important to me to create something *pleasing* or something *meaningful?*

☞ Looking forward, what is most important to me? Even though it might be painful at first, what new choices will help me feel more aligned in my integrity?

*What has been set down in a moment of ardor
must now be critically examined.*

—Pyotr Ilyich Tchaikovsky

If Passion drives, let Reason hold the Reins.

—Benjamin Franklin

*Judgment . . . is not ruthless, but steady and
obsessed by the search for truth.*

—J. Ruth Gendler

Judgment

JUDGMENT . . . it's a scary word. Sensitive by nature, many creators may still feel haunted by images of a parent or authority figure wagging a disapproving finger. Over the years, I've had more than one client whose dreams were interrupted by the reverberating refrain of a stern lecture: *"What's the matter with you? Why did you do that? If you hadn't done that, I wouldn't have to say this to you!"* Followed by the face-saving conceit, *"You know, I am only telling you this for your own good."*

Just typing those words makes me shudder.

As a young woman, I resist my yearning to write and paint because I fear doing it wrong and being criticized. In contrast, I feel more comfortable discussing and exchanging ideas. Furthermore, I have perfected the art of bolstering a weak position with flashy bravado.

If I say something with enough authority, I can be mighty convincing. But put it down on paper and there it sits, naked and defenseless—a tangible, permanent, and inviting target.

I come from a family where judgments were passed around the table along with the plate of dinner rolls. Growing up, I needed to be fast with a retort in order to defend against the almost constant barrage of critical commentary that passed for conversation in our household. As much as I hated being the object of one of my father's passionate diatribes, I learned to defend my positions while taking stands on everything from puberty to politics. Only much later did I realize that the power and strength that self-righteous opinions afforded me could also prove creatively self-defeating.

······· ·•

The problem with being *judgmental*—besides the fact that you end up alienating a lot of people—is the damage it does to your own psyche. Creative juices tend to dry up when one part of your mind loudly pontificates, controls, evaluates, demands, or criticizes while the other part wants to play, experiment, and explore. At the same time, you can't create without the ability to express a point of view, make decisions, plan, compartmentalize, and discriminate—all of which come under the purview of *good judgment*.

Just as a rush to judgment can seriously impede creative expression, so too can lack of judgment. Passion and imagination lie at the core of good work, but rarely carry a creator through the rigors of the journey. The world is full of talented people whose best ideas never emerge from the shadows. Where passion and imagination overwhelm judgment, a paralysis of initiative frequently follows.

Judgment plays a complex role in the creative process. Despite its much maligned potential to suffocate and damage the human spirit, judgment can evolve into a creator's closest ally and partner. Properly restrained and channeled, judgment provides invaluable structure and illuminating intelligence in support of the creative impulse.

······•

How can I turn the destructive megalomaniacal tendencies of my judgmental mind into a supportive team player? Of course such a radical transformation will not happen by itself. You must take the initiative by turning towards and standing up to the *critical* judge within, instead of seeking refuge in the nearest pint of Häagen-Dazs. Rather than running to your favorite escape, take your critical judge in hand and tell that bully, in no uncertain terms, "Your behavior is not helping." Then instruct your critical judge on how his or her considerable powers are to be used. Instead of squashing, censoring, disparaging, and generally demoralizing you, an *enlightened* judge will aspire to a higher standard.

Throughout the process, judgment shapes and tempers (but never overwhelms) creative inspiration. An *objective* judge suspends criticism during the early stages, leaving our childlike nature free to soar on the wings of imagination. A friend has a daughter who cannot yet read or write but already tells stories. Mom writes them down without changing a word, nodding and encouraging (not correcting grammatical errors) as the little girl bubbles over with enthusiasm. Like a loving parent or teacher, we must learn to simply observe and record our own imaginative ramblings.

After periods of intuitive discovery and experimentation, a *shrewd* judge helps us to weigh the alternatives and decide which of the many promising paths are worth pursuing. When information overload, setbacks, and ensuing demands threaten to overwhelm our sensibilities, we can rely on judgment's *wisdom* to re-frame the situation from a calmer perspective.

We also need judgment to analyze the conditions that enable the creative side of our nature to flourish and produce good work. A *discerning* judge knows your strengths and weaknesses and uses that knowledge, not to ridicule or criticize, but to help you succeed. Think about how you like to work, when you like to work, and what helps you to feel free inside. Do you need a quiet workspace? What about more time for creative ambitions? Judgment's penchant for *discipline* helps you to control your environment, resist tempting distractions, and stick with the difficult concessions that enable you to achieve your dreams.

When we work passionately, a *respectful* judge honors the magic of engagement and the sanctity of intuitive flow. Judgment may some-times whisper suggestions or reminders to stop and eat, but while we are absorbed in work, a *humble* judge remains in the background, always reserving serious critical commentary for a later date.

Good judgment works as a partner throughout the creative journey; but during the final phases of editing and critiquing, judgement's *analytical* skills take center stage. What has been received and executed in a soul-stirring moment of passion must now be evaluated, fine tuned, polished, checked and double-checked.

······ · ··●

Evaluating your work requires great delicacy. You need to be able to see where something succeeds and where it doesn't. You also need impeccable honesty. Learning to engage in an honest dialogue with yourself will help you grow creatively. Creators who never confront the deficiencies in their work stagnate. Relentless optimism blinds you to legitimate problems in your work, which prevents you from making improvements. Ask yourself: *Wouldn't I rather notice these problems before somebody else does?*

At the same time, you need to respect that you are a fallible human being who has taken a wisp of inspiration (along with a hope and a prayer) and dreamed it, shaped it, and brought it to life; you have struggled and poured your heart into something you love. You need to value that effort, even if it doesn't always produce the results you had hoped.

A *dispassionate* judge acknowledges problems without being overly critical. Attacking your work or your character doesn't accomplish anything except to discourage you from ever trying again. You aren't stupid or hopeless just because your work has flaws. That sort of harsh self-judgment comes from fear and should be rejected as such. *If you want to improve the quality of your work, separate your self-worth from the piece you have made.* Your creation might contain errors, but that doesn't mean you and your entire life are defective. Remember what the writer James Joyce once said: "Errors are portals to discovery."

······∙•

What criteria should I use for evaluating my creative work? It isn't a question of whether your work is right or wrong—creativity isn't a math test—but how honest you have been, how well the work succeeds in communicating its intention or in solving the problem, and what you need to do technically to bring it into alignment if it does not. Above all, you must ask yourself, *Does it have resonance?* (When something works it feels right on a gut level, as if something has fallen into its proper place.)

Make specific, actionable recommendations when evaluating your work. Sweeping generalizations such as "This piece is really boring" or "I hate it" do not lead to improvement. Be specific. What precisely do you dislike so intensely and why? What reaction arises inside you? And then, instead of beating yourself up about it, *offer some constructive suggestions for making improvements.* If none are forthcoming resist the urge to hack your piece to bits and use it as kindling. You likely will need to step back from the project before you can see it with objective eyes. When you're finished working, just put it away for a while. You'll know when it's time to take it out again for modifications.

······ ··•

Personally, when I start examining my work, I have some pretty counterproductive thoughts. It's natural to compare our efforts with others' and find ourselves coming up short. Great writers create prose so dazzling that I practically weep with envy. What's more, I fear in my heart of hearts that I can never be *that* good. Not ever.

In my more constructive moments, I focus on the basics; I try to do the best I can. I go back and reread earlier pages and think, "I like the way this section sounds: honest, heartfelt, and clear . . . but that paragraph I've rewritten three times still doesn't work."

Here's the thing: It's really, *really* hard to give up on being perfect and just be ourselves. But once we accept ourselves as we are, we can take our work deeper and farther. We can grow our character and talent by risking new directions, emphasizing our strengths, and working to advance our technical limitations.

Harsh and unforgiving judgments will not make us better creators; the only alternative is to fairly assess what we need to do to improve our work and then endeavor to do it. Coming to terms with the judgmental side of our nature frees us to accept criticism which, in the long run, makes us better creators. We need no longer fear the judgment of others once we have befriended our own.

Further Reflections On Judgment

Judgment steadies your resolve to work faithfully toward truth. If you wish to go deeper, explore one or more of the following questions. *Write, draw, dance, paint, meditate . . .*

☞ What role does critical thinking play in my creative process? How do I use constructive criticism to improve my work?

☞ How can I prevent critical thinking from deteriorating into self-criticism?

☞ What if I stop asking *subjective* questions that invariably lead to self-admonishment: Is it good enough? Am I good enough? Will anyone like it?

☞ What if I start asking *objective* questions: Does it solve the problem? What works? What doesn't? What improvements can I make? Is this the best I can do even if it isn't perfect? Are there other resources I can consider that will get me closer to my desired outcome?

☞ How might I reframe my self-judgments? Hint: Look for hidden strengths in areas of weakness.

☞ All this makes a lot of sense, but my inner judge is out of control. Is it time to get outside assistance to help rehabilitate my inner judge?

Which is the work in which [a creator] hasn't
surrendered, under dire difficulty, the best thing he
meant to have kept?

—Henry James

We're only as great as our ability to negotiate
with our limitations.

—Abigail Washburn

Sometimes you're gonna maneuver, you're gonna give
a little to survive. But selling out means accepting
goals and tactics of society as your own . . . when you
don't agree with that way of life at all.

—Michael Ventura

Compromise

I REMEMBER LISTENING to a radio interview with a famous author who had published a wildly successful novel. I don't recall the name of the writer or her book, but the interview has stuck in my mind all these years because of the writer's ambiguous feelings about her own success. Oddly enough, she said she was not altogether happy because her editor had removed what the writer considered "the most profound parts of my book." No matter if she was receiving good reviews for the book, no matter if the editor actually made it a better book, the writer was still bemoaning the compromises she had felt compelled to make.

I can empathize with the writer's sense of loss. Sometimes I become so connected to a piece of work that to alter it in any way seems tantamount to losing an old friend. I tend to be nostalgic about material things as well. It takes all the conscious determination I can muster to get rid of something that no longer serves me. I feel attached to its beauty, the quality of workmanship, or the memory it evokes.

Creators cannot afford sentimental self-indulgence. When it comes to revising, we need to be bold about making concessions that strengthen the work. For the sake of the greater good, we must take a deep breath, pick up the surgeon's scalpel—or in some cases an ax—and cut out whatever weakens the other elements . . .

The other night, my friend Seth shared an inspiring story about the agonies and rewards of creative compromise.

"I had been working on the second in a series of small metal sculptures. The first piece worked beautifully so I thought I was onto something. I had this idea that chain mail would hang like a bird's nest inside a silver container I had made. I really loved the concept. And I spent many, many tedious hours trying to make it work. But I discovered that even though the idea fit perfectly in my mind, in reality, the execution left a lot to be desired. Each element was so beautiful in itself; yet the marriage between them created an awkward and cumbersome combination. *The truth was staring me in the face but I could not accept it.* I clung to the notion that they belonged together—they needed each other. I kept trying and trying to break the impasse. Finally, I had to give up and just let the container stand alone. I was really frustrated at having to make that concession—but I sent it to be judged for a national design competition anyway. I just couldn't believe it when it won FIRST place. It's funny, but I still have that piece of chain mail. Twenty years later, it sits on a shelf; I never did find a place for it."

Seth's story illustrates an important aesthetic consideration: Every element in a piece of work must be at home, must take its place alongside the others, each part supporting the whole. Sometimes the only way you can save your work, move it forward, or raise it up, is to make the hard compromises—and embrace the kind of heart-tugging sacrifice that elevated Seth's metal piece to a national prizewinner.

······•

Creators who demand perfection, who lack the flexibility to make adjustments in their expectations, will rarely finish anything. Sadly, the quixotic quest for perfection eventually turns into an irritable dissatisfaction that condemns a creator to wander endlessly in a baffling maze, searching for an absolute ideal that can only exist in the mind's eye.

Of course, you will always keep seeing how your work could be better, and probably it could be. Nagging anxiety may compel you to keep tinkering and tweaking, cutting and pasting, twisting and turning, until you change something that you think will improve the piece. At first, it seems to, but when you come back to it later, you can't really tell anymore whether it's been improved. At some point, continuous striving collapses into creative exhaustion.

On the eve of completion, compromise asks you to find a way to live comfortably within this confounding, infuriating paradox: Even though you've done your best, at some level you may never feel it's quite good enough. And you need to let go anyway.

······•

Base your criteria for completion in reality. Unrealistic and unattainable standards will only frustrate you and eventually strip your creative work of its energy and appeal. Passionate ideals set you off on your journey, but now you need to compromise within the limits of your talent, skill, and better judgment.

Often what we envision lies beyond our technical ability. I'm not completely happy with this book. All along I've had to contend with the limits of my style, language, and storytelling abilities. Rather than get hung up on that, I also need to acknowledge the merits of this book— while recognizing that it isn't going to be the last thing I will ever write.

You can't accomplish everything you want in any single piece. Don't put all your hopes and ambitions into one outcome and then drive yourself crazy trying to perfect it. Van Gogh painted sunflowers and haystacks over and over again. And, how many ways did Monet depict that same lily pond or Degas portray those ballerinas? At some point you just have to say, "I've done my best on this one." In the next project you can make adjustments, apply the learning you have gained from the previous attempt, and try again.

······ ·· ●

We frequently think of compromise as a concession we make in order to get along with others or to appease the tastes and demands of the marketplace. Perhaps that is why the famous author I heard on the radio spoke so mournfully about her loss. Perhaps what she considered her best writing had to be condensed to make the final product commercially viable.

Given the choice between completing work that only a few of your closest friends will see and the opportunity to reach a larger audience, most of us will gladly make accommodations for the chance to step up to the next level. A movie director may reshoot a controversial scene in order to get an NC-17-rating changed to one that will appeal to a wider audience, or an architect may back away from a design he knows will be judged as too esoteric by a client (even though the architect regards it as an excellent solution). It is a rare creator who can afford to please no one but him or herself.

Whenever you are part of a creative team or when someone else pays the bills, compromise plays a central role. The client may have specific needs or price constraints and you have to take them into account. Even though you envision an edgier upscale option, you may feel pressured—or you may pressure yourself—to tamp it down so that your work fits the client's conservative palate and budget. Contrary to what some creative purists advocate, compromising within constraints imposed by other people need not diminish your work. In fact, it can make it better.

Collaboration necessitates compromise. Creators with outsized egos, who refuse to modify their "holy" vision, do themselves and their work—not to mention their audience and clients—a disservice. "Your work can always be improved," says a Hollywood screenwriter and producer who has mentored dozens of young writers. "If you have the attitude that your work is perfect, then you become someone who can't work with other people in a productive way," she says. "You just end up isolating yourself and frustrating your creativity in the long run."

Choreographer Myles Thatcher echoes this dynamic and inclusive perspective on compromise. Thatcher states that creative vitality flows from "allowing dancers to challenge me with their own points of view." The most productive moments occur when creators remain receptive, "when we can all challenge each other and something that's bigger than all of us manifests."

······ ·· ●

In the light of personal integrity, where do I draw the line with unacceptable compromise? When possible, educate the people around you so they can understand how your vision helps solve their problem or meet their needs. Taking a proactive position can help prevent an unacceptable compromise. But it is equally important to ask why your idea or approach is being questioned. Are you too close to the work to be objective? What bigger picture may you be failing to recognize?

How can I do my best work if I make more money doing less than my best? Many creators sidestep this difficult issue by having some other means, aside from their art, to pay the bills. Even if you do not have that luxury, there must be some line you refuse to cross. Whatever fortune or recognition is obtained by selling yourself short, it may not be worth it in the end. A designer told me that no matter how lean times are, he never accepts work from unappreciative clients whose only criterion is the bottom line. "More times than not, those clients will recommend me to friends who want the same sort of unimaginative work—and that's the last thing I need."

There is a huge difference between *compromise* and *selling out*. Success that results from making unacceptable compromises is a dubious achievement at best. At worst, it smothers your passion and engenders discontent. Without a place to stand, you will eventually be cast adrift in your own despair.

The *art* of compromise brings good judgment together with inspiration, passionate idealism, and marketing savvy. As a creator, you will invariably make compromises for a variety of reasons. However, in the final analysis, the best compromises are those that propel your work farther than you ever imagined it could go.

Further Reflections On Compromise

Are you a compromiser or a controller? If you wish to go deeper, explore one or more of the following questions. *Write, draw, dance, paint, meditate . . .*

➥ Can I set aside my ego and do what's best for the project?

☞ What is the role of compromise in ensuring a successful collaboration? Can I give up ownership of my ideas and create new solutions that work better for everyone?

☞ Do I compromise too easily? How can I sense when standing firm is the best course of action?

☞ What *unacceptable* compromises have I made in the past? How does that experience affect my ability to recognize creative compromises that might benefit me today? Upon reflection, were those compromises truly unacceptable or did I let my ego blind me to necessary improvements?

☞ What am I struggling to complete right now? What, specifically, frightens me about completing a project or moving on to the next stage?

☞ Where do I resist compromise as a strategy to avoid completion?

☞ What compromises may I need to accept as part of the price for completion? What stops me from accepting them? What might happen if I let go?

*We sum ourselves up, giving blessings and receiving
them: We practice the language of fulfillment.*

—Cassandra Light

*I had the virtuous tiredness that comes when you've
done something demanding but healthy and feel
entitled to rest.*

—Jon Katz

*The only peace, the only security,
is in fulfillment.*

—Henry Miller

Fulfillment

AHHHHH . . . Is there anything more delicious than basking in the languorous warmth mixed with relief of a job well done? It is our soul savoring its own fulfillment. Unfortunately, too many of us barely touch down long enough to acknowledge our efforts and achievements, let alone feel deeply nourished by them.

With the prospect of completion looming, creators often worry, hurry, and hustle in anticipation of whatever project comes next. Future-gazing can be a comforting and exciting activity; but it can also be distracting and addicting. If we become too preoccupied with what's on the horizon, we may miss or diminish what lies right in front of us—our moment of arrival. When we lose the meaning and import of such a precious moment, we lose a part of ourselves as well. Separated from the fullness of completion, we have stripped

the process—as well as our accomplishment—of its significance
and value.

•••••·'··•

I am thinking about the explorer Meriwether Lewis. The visionary
leader of the Lewis and Clark Expedition crossed thousands of miles
through unknown territory, faced down innumerable dangers, while
creatively spearheading solutions to the challenges of disease, deprivation, and desertion—all in the midst of negotiating with the native
inhabitants—in order to realize the vision of a continental United States.

Imagine the moment Lewis and his small scouting party finally reach
a high pass through the rugged Rocky Mountains: to the east, a snow-
capped wall of solid granite; to the west, a panorama of mountains
receding into the distance as far as the eye can see. It would seem an
incomparable arrival—to be the first American of European ancestry
to stand at the northern Continental Divide.

Sadly, Meriwether Lewis experienced only an incompleteness that
transcended the supreme moment of his achievement; an achievement
as momentous in its day as Neil Armstrong's first step on the moon. In
the end, he became preoccupied with the expedition's minor failures
and wrote: "I have done nothing of any significance with my life."

As creators, we too leave the familiar in order to blaze new trails and
climb peaks of possibility. Uncertainty and struggle assail us, but if we
persevere we are rewarded with the glorious fulfillment of arrival, of
accomplishing what we set out to do. Ask yourself: *How often do I scale
my own peaks, only to find, like Meriwether Lewis, that I am unable to feel
satisfied, let alone plant my flag and claim my own good work?*

•••••·'··•

A creator feels validated by action, by the powerful adrenalin rush of getting things done. But we need to be careful not to allow our preoccupation with *doing* to cause us to bypass the quieter moments in the creative process, when we need to cease our relentless participation, let go, and invite in the emotional fruits of our creative labors.

As exciting as the activity of creative problem-solving can be, running headlong into the next project sends a message to ourselves (whether or not we are aware of it) that we aren't worth very much. *In such cases, doing more can actually feel like less.* Eventually, our creative spirit despairs and resists going forward. "Why bother? No matter what I do, it's never enough." After a while, the only thing that can germinate and blossom in such a barren environment is the bitter root of resentment.

Dana shares this dispiriting experience common to many successful clients. An overachiever, she suffers from a deep sense of exhaustion, a symptom I have observed in clients who don't realize they may also be depressed. Dana wants to "feel more pleasure" in her accomplishments. At the same time, she expresses annoyance at having to make any adjustments "that will take time away from all the important projects I need to be working on." Dana has trapped herself in the demands of a creative life that leave little room for the emotional nourishment she needs in order to maintain a healthy balance between giving and receiving. *Does Dana's dilemma feel familiar to you?*

·····ː··●

To feel *fulfilled* means to have the emotional experience of feeling *full* or *filled up*. Being able to experience this sense of inner fullness has everything to do with *the capacity to receive love*.

But how can we feel fulfilled or loved when we are constantly thinking about something else, planning, problem-solving, or consumed

by tasks? We need time and space to notice, understand, and respond
to what we are feeling in our bodies. The hectic pace of productivity
becomes numbing; it practically compels us to stay in our heads and
construct lives without room for connection to deeper feeling. If we
merely make and do things; if we only focus on the practicalities of
technique, goals, or results; if we are not also using the creative process
as an opportunity to go deeper, to heal ourselves, and value our unique
gifts while feeling connected to something larger than ourselves; then
we may end up, like Dana, never reaping the inner riches of connection
and fulfillment—no matter what we outwardly accomplish.

······⸱··●

Some people consider emotional unrest a "blessed state" that ensures
creative vitality by continually pushing creators to reinvent themselves
and their work. Martha Graham, the flamboyant pioneer of modern
dance, subscribed to this popular notion. She once famously remarked,
"There is no satisfaction whatever at any time . . . only a queer divine
dissatisfaction that keeps us [creators] marching and makes us more
alive than the others." As I write this, I can't help but also think of
the inevitable cliché of the tortured artist self-destructing in the service of genius and talent. The romantic view that great art can only be
made by creators who are troubled or perpetually discontented seems
outmoded in this age of recovery and twelve-step programs.

Emotional fulfillment does not inevitably lead to a kind of creative
death. The superstition against feeling *too good* has to do with the
fear of losing our creative edge. Satisfaction, however, needn't be at
odds with the instinctive drive for creative renewal—it's simply one
of many emotions we cycle through while birthing our creations. So
we might as well show ourselves a little love and bask in fulfillment's
warm glow while we can.

Fulfillment and love inexorably intertwine. When you finish your work, pause long enough to savor the fullness of the moment, realize that what you've done matters—that you matter. And then, find some way to celebrate. Ask yourself: *Do I love myself enough to grant myself the inner peace of fulfillment?*

Creative fulfillment provides both a point of completion . . . and a point of departure, a launching place for a new beginning. By allowing the fruit of fulfillment to nourish us, we lay the groundwork and build the confidence to see us through the next phase of the journey. Or perhaps, strengthen ourselves to begin a new one.

Further Reflections On Fulfillment

The joy of fulfillment inspires you to act beyond your long list of failings. If you wish to go deeper, explore one or more of the following questions. *Write, draw, dance, paint, meditate . . .*

☞ Do I pause long enough to experience the fullness of completion? Or do I minimize my progress by demanding more and more from myself?

☞ In what ways do I block positive feelings for fear of becoming creatively stale and stagnant?

☞ If I judge myself as undeserving, how does this judgment affect my ability to finish what I start?

☞ When I celebrate my accomplishments with others does it seem like I am sharing—or bragging?

☞ What has it taken for me to come this far? How might I celebrate?

Hard on the heels of these self-congratulations,
however, came the deeply disquieting feeling of
emptiness and disorientation.

—Peter London

What will happen with this great empty space that
I am today? What will fill me now that not a whiff
of ambition remains?

—Isabel Allende

There is a time for the labor of digging and mixing
earths, a time for the heat of fire, and a time for
contemplating what is done.

—Celia Davis Cunningham

Emptiness

MORNING LIGHT BREAKS above the ridge as I prepare to sit down and
work on these pages. Quite unexpectedly, the phone rings. My client
Selena urgently inquires: "Are you busy? I've got to talk to you NOW!"

"Of course," I answer. "You're up early this morning. What's going on?"

"I-I-I-d-d-d-o-n-'t really know." Selena chokes back tears. "I have
these feelings of panic and sadness and emptiness all at the same time.
I should be happy and excited, shouldn't I? What's wrong?"

It seemed like only yesterday that Selena and I were celebrating.
She had finally completed enough work for her one-woman show. The
last time we met, Selena practically glided through my door, radiating
an easy warmth and self-satisfied glow: "You won't believe it!" she
exclaimed excitedly. "I finished late last night. I'm done!"

But a few short weeks later, after all the celebrating and hearty congratulations, after the relief of "having my life back" and an end to those all-nighters in the studio, it suddenly hits Selena—the creative relationship that has occupied her thoughts and dreams, the creative goal that has filled up her days, giving shape and focus and significance to her life, has ended. "All I feel is this exhaustion and a weird sense of being let down. Does that make any sense?"

Indeed it does.

······∙∙∙●

We expect completion to invigorate us, and for a short time it does. But Selena's confusion illustrates the anticlimactic quality that often characterizes completion. As much as we want to hold onto the sanguine blush and self-satisfaction of fulfillment, inevitably these feelings fade, just as they did for Selena.

Once we complete a run of productive work or reach an important goal, those *good* feelings can't last forever. Instead, they frequently give way to an uneasy feeling of emptiness that settles in the pit of the stomach. A creator realizes, with a horror that is only occasionally redeemed by a profound sense of irony, "I have done *all of this work*, only to be thrust once again into the void. Is this some kind of existential joke?!! Now what?"

Selena invested many years of her life working to fulfill a dream. She made painful personal sacrifices to reach her destination. And despite the difficulties, she hasn't questioned her decision until now— *only after she has achieved her goal*. In many ways, Selena is experiencing a kind of postpartum letdown. She has just given birth successfully. Now, exhausted from the effort, she needs to recover.

·····⸱··•

When you invest so much of yourself in something that matters, feelings of emptiness frequently replace the intensity of anticipation and effort. The project you've devoted your energy to has been like a friend, a lover, a child, or a protector. With completion, the project no longer supports you or your sense of who you are. That void can feel like an abandonment. The familiar and insulating routines, the excitement of discovery and breakthrough, the potency of engagement—even the problems and tensions—were part of an ongoing connection. So along with feelings of satisfaction, completion brings a certain vulnerability—an unsettling disruption in your identity and sense of purpose.

After the fulfillment of finishing and before finding the next project, creators enter a transition period that lacks tangible structure—*this formless transition space registers as emptiness in the body.* Some creators feel liberated in the void, relishing emptiness as a place to relax or find inspiration. Others become restless, anxious, and despondent, filling the space with premonitions of doom or frenetic activity.

·····⸱··•

While something may end in terms of linear time, its presence, meaning, and effect continue to be held by the body. From a creative perspective, emptiness provides a nourishing space for reflection. Through *creative reflection* you support the process of detachment and calm the nervous discomforts of emptiness. Over time, this practice softens your mind, allowing your creative spirit to unfold and deepen. You will find the intimacy of a reflective mind a refreshing contrast to the kind of sharp critical thinking that helps you revise and edit work. *Remember, rather than continuing to look for errors to fix or ways to improve your piece, your purpose during creative reflection is simply to commune.*

·····˙··●

If fulfillment accompanies completion and the celebration of its attainment, reflection within emptiness honors what you have made and understands it at a deeper level. In reflection, you focus tender attention on the thing you have brought to life for the sole purpose of meeting it as if for the first time.

Just as a new mother stares into the eyes of her infant, creators who want to feel nurtured by their efforts need to commune with their own work while asking the question: *Who are you?*

I explain to Selena, "Even if you have spent much of your waking moments consumed by your work, in some ways it still remains unfamiliar to you." Similarly, we can live for years and years in close proximity to our mates and believe we understand their every idiosyncrasy—yet in other ways, they remain virtual strangers to us.

During our phone conversation, Selena reminds me that she still needs to compose her artist's statement. It will be the perfect opportunity for those feelings of emptiness and vulnerability to become a gateway for personal reflection.

At our next meeting, I ask Selena what her work has meant to her: "What is it about?" At first, she doesn't know what to say. "I feel totally empty. What have I been doing for all these years, anyway?"

I suggest she stand each piece up in a circle around the room and sit down in the center. Selena takes a step back. She finds it awkward to place herself in such close proximity to her work without, as she states, "actually doing something to it."

I wait and watch as Selena makes her decision. Slowly, she moves each painting into position, leaning the last one against a low bank of windows. Outside, a blossoming crabapple tree arches gracefully in the distance.

Selena and I sit together in a corner of the room, taking in the full measure of her efforts. The visual experience startles as we encounter her oversized constructions—splashes of color spilling over and off the edges, twisted pieces, disturbing yet hauntingly beautiful. Each reflects a part of Selena's soul. Time passes . . . I hear Selena take a slow in-breath, and then silence. Her quiet tears fall easily now. Slowly, Selena rises and moves to the center of the circle. Entering the core of her emptiness, Selena has, at last, come home.

·······•

You may find it difficult to enter into emptiness for the purpose of reflection, but the rewards of savoring the deeper import of what you do as a creator will make it well worth the effort. Much about your process and your work remains unknowable until you are finished. One special reward remains hidden until the last moment, like a Christmas package you stumble upon in a closet, weeks after all the other gifts have been unwrapped. This quiet discovery surprises all the more for its belated arrival. Weeks, months, or sometimes, years later, you need to consider what you have done—what it is and what it means.

At the heart of our work lie the revelations, experiences, trials, and tribulations that can become a source of wisdom and inspiration—provided we take the time to reflect on the journey in its entirety. In so doing, we move beyond the merits of the product to focus on the deeper picture. Certainly, we cannot make a journey of this magnitude and come to the end of it unchanged. The person we have become at the end of the process has evolved from the person we were when we started. Let us embrace emptiness as reflective space, a quiet place where we can commune and meet ourselves anew.

Further Reflections On Emptiness

When you are finished, really finished, sit quietly facing your work. If you wish to go deeper, explore one or more of the following questions. *Write, draw, dance, paint, meditate . . .*

☞ Did I hold anything back? Where could I have dug a little deeper?

☞ Have I been true to myself and my vision?

☞ Was I afraid to venture into certain areas? If so, what were they?

☞ What risks did I take? Where did I go that I never imagined I would? What surprised me?

☞ What have I learned? How can I improve next time?

☞ In what ways have I grown or evolved? What qualities of character have revealed themselves as a result of my process?

☞ What has this journey meant to me?

☞ Am I ready to move on?

You take a final step and, look, suddenly
You're there. You've arrived . . .
Now, what you make of it means everything.

—*David Wagoner*

*Man unites himself with the world in the
process of creation.*

—Eric Fromm

*Steppin' out with my baby. Can't go wrong
'cause I'm in right. Ask me when will the day
be, the big day may be tonight.*

—Irving Berlin

*Sometimes, you wish you could go back . . .
but up there onstage, exactly where you always
wanted to be, you must simply find your way.*

—Jeremy Denk

7
Stepping
Out

WHEN YOU HAVE FINALLY COMPLETED your work and feel ready to share, it's time to let go and send your baby out into the world. Unfortunately, you have to go out there and keep it company. Taking this step can become a source of extreme anxiety for creators more comfortable with making something than with showing or selling.

Why does the thought of stepping out cause so many creators to turn and run for cover? Perhaps because our creations become bound up with our perceptions of ourselves, and that makes our self-esteem vulnerable to marketplace fluctuations.

Stepping Out is the stage in the creative process when the creator's heart meets the world. Creators need a strong foundation built on experience, patient struggle, and self confidence to withstand the pressures of public scrutiny. Alternatively, unbridled fear focused in the right direction can be the fuel that propels you across this final threshold.

More than once in my life a little *desperate courage* has plunged me into new circumstances with positive results.

Remember, you never ever have to step out. You don't need the approval of an audience to enjoy the deeply satisfying experience of having poured your heart and soul into something you care about, something that is uniquely yours. A creative life can be a private pleasure—a quiet communion. Working out of the limelight, to paraphrase the artist Mark Rothko, can be a "golden time" with nothing to lose and a vision to gain.

Of course, when you do pour your heart and soul into something that really matters, you may start to get restless for feedback. You may want the world to see this marvelous thing you've created. You may want your work to make a difference in the lives of others. Asking for attention can be an important part of the creative process. Ask yourself: *Do I feel compelled to share an important experience, message, or idea? Do I want recognition for my efforts?* If so, you may need to take your baby beyond the safe haven of your home, office, or studio.

Despite the dangers inherent in exposing ourselves to the indifference or outright hostility of the world, we choose to embrace these hazards for the sake of connection. Our work remains a solitary encounter until we offer it up with the fervent hope that someone somewhere will receive it.

Qualities that strengthen the connection between the creator and the audience include *communication, transparency, standing place, success,* and *gratitude*.

Communication forms a meaningful exchange between us and the audience vis-à-vis our work. *Transparency* allows our gifts to be seen and shared. *Standing Place* establishes a foundation from which to take on the marketplace. *Success* results from the communication of our vision and any ensuing rewards. *Gratitude* gives thanks for the opportunities we have been given.

*If there is no communication it is as though
the work has been stillborn.*

—Madeleine L'Engle

*I feel that special current between the public
and me. . . . That is a great, great moment.*

—Arthur Rubenstein

*[Creativity] is a way of communicating vision and
experience so that it reaches beyond a single moment in
time. What fills our hearts and spills over must be shared.*

—Stormy Bailey

Communication

EVEN IF NOTHING IS MORE IMPORTANT or honorable than finding your
own meaning in what you do, the creative process may feel incomplete
unless you can engage in some sort of dialogue about it with others.
Communicating with an audience (or consumer) allows creators, in the
words of essayist Susan Griffin, to "move the gift."

With this spirit of generosity in mind, my friends and I decide to
plan our own art reception. It will be the first time I display my paintings for everyone to see. We send out a hundred invitations that feature
our Gang of Five artists nervously peeking out from a closet, just on
the brink of stepping out.

On the day before the big event, we empty Jeff's house of every
stick of furniture and transform it into a fantastic gallery space, filling
it inside and out with food and wine, flowers, and art. Lots and lots

of art. We design the event as a delight for the senses. Every room overflows with paintings, drawings, sculpture, photographs, and music—we even offer a theatrical performance. More than two hundred people jam themselves into the house and garden.

Later that night, Susan calls to inquire about buying one of my pieces. It turns out that she is in the process of recovering from a head-on collision with a drunken driver that broke numerous bones in her body and put her in a coma for months. During Susan's convalescence in the hospital, she experienced periods of delirium in which she kept "mumbling something about the color *teal*." After a year of physical therapy, she now can walk with a cane. Susan says the doctors considered her survival a miracle. On the afternoon of the reception, Susan found herself mesmerized by one of my "Soul Portraits"—a misshapen, blue-faced Amazon I had named "Teal Woman," proudly seated on a red throne. For a moment, Susan wondered if it had been painted for her as a testament to her own endurance.

Frankly, I had to wonder too.

When creative work communicates to others, it transcends the creator's private vision and speaks to a reality beyond the purely personal. Listening to Susan's story, I was struck by the staggering synchronicity of our connection. I had never met Susan before. Where had that inspiration come from and how had it managed to find its way to the perfect buyer? As creators in search of an audience, we sometimes have the honor of becoming important links in a chain of truth.

······ꞏ··●

As humans, we have a natural drive to communicate. To a large extent our survival depends on connecting our inner landscape of imagination, feeling, and thought with the outer world. I am reminded of the book *The Diving Bell and the Butterfly,* written by Jean-Dominique

Bauby, a vibrant man in the prime of life who became trapped in his body after suffering a stroke. Paralyzed, except for the use of his left eye, he blinked each letter of each word in each sentence and managed to create a remarkable narrative—heroically communicating beyond the confines of his inner life.

Few fates seem as terrifying as his—being cut off from all communication while in possession of a fully functioning mind. He likened it to being trapped in a diving bell. Yet when I read the author's story, what I experienced was not a suffocating feeling of claustrophobia, but rather a soaring sense of the miraculous. He found a way, however awkward and time consuming, to transform private despair into a celebration of life. It is perhaps more than an interesting coincidence that two days after the book's publication, the author died. Communication was the final purpose of his life.

······· •

Many creators spend long hours working alone. Without someone to receive those efforts, the creative process can become isolating. "It sometimes feels like I am standing at the edge of a precipice shouting a lonely cry into the void," an artist friend remarked. Without an audience do our creations fully exist? Do we? With no one to bear witness, do our efforts become like a tree falling in a forest that no one hears? When we have something to say, no matter what form our expressions take, capturing the interest of another human being can provide important validation.

The instinct for feedback starts before we can talk. Babies lock onto their parents' eyes; they cry for recognition. Their existence seems to depend on this exchange of energy. And later, when the freedom of mobility carries us as toddlers to the edge of a new world, we can't wait to share. Perhaps we find a shiny black bug with skinny legs, or a bit of dirt we mix with water and cleverly pack into a cup. Impulsively, we come running into the house, trailing muddy footprints, thrusting our precious gift at Mother, in the midst of a quiet lunch. *"LOOK! LOOK AT THIS!!!"* We can't understand why Mom doesn't find this bug as fascinating as we do or appreciate those interesting clumps of mud clinging to her china. And why does her silly carpet matter so much anyway?

How quickly we lose our innocence. How quickly we learn that just because something excites us, it doesn't guarantee that others will share our joy. And so it begins: the delight of discovery, the longing to share, and the struggle to be recognized.

When we present our creations, we are, at one level, as innocent as children. We offer up gifts from the deepest part of ourselves, and that is an incredibly risky act. And because we cannot predict how our offerings will be received, and because we have all been wounded by previous attempts, it is also an incredibly courageous act. That we can still maintain such hope after so much loss is, like that man blinking missives from inside a diving bell, an act that celebrates the resilience of the human spirit.

·····‥·•

Creators take a formless idea, bring it to life, and send it out into the world. When it is received and a response sent in return, that exchange opens us to a wider field of possibility. We may experience the mind-blowing, heartwarming, soul-satisfying gratification of having reached down into ourselves for something dear that ends up touching, transporting, or enriching someone's life.

But, it is also possible that your attempt to communicate may miss the mark, hit a little too accurately for some to handle, or arrive at the wrong time. You may encounter rejection, misunderstanding, indifference, or even hostility. Although painful, this kind of feedback can still be useful if you are willing to learn from the encounter. In the long run, missed communications can give you vital knowledge about yourself, strengthen your determination, and help you focus on areas that need improvement. Stepping out to communicate your vision furthers the discovery process that first inspired the journey.

Further Reflections On Communication

Do you find more value in the creative process as a personal encounter or as a means of communication with the outside world? If you wish to go deeper, explore one or more of the following questions. *Write, draw, dance, paint, meditate . . .*

☞ How important is it for me to find an audience for my work? If only a few people see my work would that be okay, or do I want to attract wide attention?

☞ Is my work accessible; can others understand its meaning or is it too esoteric or too personal?

☞ What am I withholding that needs to be communicated through my creative work? Why am I holding back? Who am I trying to please?

☞ What skills do I have or need to have that will help me navigate the marketplace? Who will help me if I don't want to do it myself?

☞ If the competitive, fast-paced marketing world isn't for me, what other means might I have for reaching an audience on my own terms?

There are people whose external reality is generous
because it is transparent, because you can read
everything, accept everything, understand everything
about them: people who carry their own sun with them.

—Carlos Fuentes

There is no persuasiveness more effectual than the
transparency of a single heart . . .

—Joseph Barber Lightfoot

We have to be ready . . . to embrace a kind of fearless
vulnerability where our transparency is our strength . . .

—Andrew Cohen

Transparency

ONCE YOU AND YOUR WORK ARE READY to be seen, it's time to locate
marketplace resources and make connections with the people who
can help. You may need a mentor who knows your creative arena
and can offer guidance, a theater company to perform your play, an
investor to finance your game-changing idea, or a publicist to help you
package yourself. Fortunately, thanks to the Internet, you now have
access to more practical, how-to information than ever before—if
you have sufficient desire and the drive to follow through. It is quite
possible that you are already drawing in energy and interest by virtue
of your own internal readiness. "When the flower opens," wrote the
fifteenth-century mystical poet Kabir, "the bees will come."

What is sometimes harder than researching, and less clear cut, is
dealing with the powerful psychological challenges that surface as you

begin to seriously consider the possibility of putting your self-esteem at risk by stepping out. The other day, my client Greg spoke eloquently about the internal pressures facing creators reluctant to take this final step: "If I meet fully with the world, I am afraid it will judge me. In that judgment, I will be swept away, devastated, emptied of everything. If I let myself be wide open, THEY will be able to convince me that I am nothing; and then everything that I know to be true and real will become false. How can I face this?"

······⋯●

Greg speaks for many of us who fear the power of criticism to call into question our self-worth, the value of our work—and, in some cases, our sense of reality. It may sometimes feel like a cruel irony that the artistic sensitivity that makes it possible to create becomes a liability when dealing with the harsh realities of the marketplace.

With so much at stake, how can I consider stepping out without some form of protection? It has often been said the best defense is a good offense, and barring that, run like hell. Indeed, we may need to safeguard our fragile egos, but too many of us take this to mean that we must encase them in a suit of armor, or at the very least, disguise them in a cloak of camouflage. In the long run, defensive solutions become problematic because they keep creators locked into self-defeating patterns.

Let's consider an alternative approach—*transparency*.

······⋯●

Transparency is a way of relating in the world without posturing or pretense, without the normal ego-defenses we consider so essential to our emotional survival. "When you are completely present, when your ego relaxes its grip, it is like a veil has been removed," writes author

Ann O'Shaughnessy. Such vulnerability feels risky, but in the long run, the power of transparency becomes one of our greatest allies in coping with the rigors of marketplace challenges.

Creators who cultivate the quality of transparency develop the ability to be totally themselves in the world, allowing themselves and their gifts to be seen and shared. They receive whatever comes their way—praise, homage, slings and arrows—with an equanimity that transcends the moment. This understated power attracts others with a sincere, heartfelt presence that says simply, "Here I am."

Instead of coming to marketplace encounters loaded down with expectations about what will happen—whether positive or negative—*we come with the attitude that we are here to give something.* And we offer it—and this is the really important part—with the understanding that *our audience has a right to refuse that gift.* We simply offer: "This is who I am. This is what I have made. This is what I feel it is worth. Here are some ways that it might benefit you and others. If we cannot come to a mutual understanding that benefits all concerned, then we are both free to move on." For an open-hearted creator, more opportunities will always arise.

······ · ··●

Revealing our gifts while armed with only our sincerity and clear intentions does not guarantee that we won't meet with setbacks, but it does enable us to survive and learn. If we are, as my client feared, "swept away" or toppled by a torrent of downturns, internal flexibility will enable us to right ourselves more quickly than rigid defensiveness.

I like that the notion of transparency offers protection without sacrificing the precious assets of sensitivity and humanity. Cultivating transparency allows us to use these qualities as a way to cushion the blow of rejection and disappointment, so that we might transform a negative situation into an opportunity for connection and further growth. A transparent heart has the power to burn through veils of deceit, pettiness, insecurity, and pretentiousness.

······ᐧᐧ●

I continually aspire to transparency, and from time to time manage to achieve it. In situations that threaten me, transparency helps me to see what is present, what needs to be dealt with, and then meet those challenges with an open heart.

I recall a huge public relations nightmare that occurred when I was consulting for several large companies. I prepared an interactive exploration on "Creative Problem Solving" using clay, music, collage, and theater games. This particular company wanted to become more competitive by encouraging a new culture of innovative thinking. In order to further this objective, an inordinate number of consultants had been brought in over the previous year.

On the day of the big event . . .

I find myself standing before the audience of senior managers. I barely get two dozen words out of my mouth when one man rises from his chair and says that he has better things to do than sit through another blankety-blank seminar. Stunned, I stop breathing and just stand there paralyzed with terror. In that instant, I fight two instinctive urges. On the one hand, I want to bolt from the room; on the other, I want to walk up to this jerk and tell him to go . . . (well, you get the idea). I feel something hard give way inside of me followed by the sensation of a sharp, tightfisted punch to my stomach as my detractor's angry words hit their mark. And then, I feel a wave of nausea. I take an involuntary step back, feeling momentarily short of breath.

Once again, I fight the powerful instinct to recoil in shame. Instead, I look directly at him. I give him my full attention: I see how his mouth pulls tightly against his face, his jutting chin unmoving, barely concealing contempt.

Terrified of being undone by his power, I take in a slow breath. Mercifully, that breath releases me and I feel something inside let go. All at once, I experience a visceral understanding: This man, along with everyone else in the room, has been told that they need to get with the new program. Their old ways of doing things are no longer valued. The attendance requirement conveys the unflattering implication that something inside them needs to be fixed. I suddenly understand why they might be just a little sick and tired of consultants.

My detractor hadn't chosen to attend my workshop. None of them had. If I wanted the event to succeed, I needed to be the one to see through the veil of resentment. I needed to recognize the man's struggle to preserve his authority and dignity. I needed to respect that even if I didn't like the way he spoke to me. I remember thinking . . .

He is not trying to deceive me. He feels diminished. Maybe, if I let him see my true intentions, we can level the playing field. . . . I soften my gaze, look him straight in the eye, and respond simply and sincerely, "I think we are all a little nervous right now, especially me. I'm not sure what you all have been going through with other consultants, but would you just please give me a chance? I promise this will be fun."

The tension, that only moments ago had threatened to suffocate any and all possibilities, had now lost some of its charge. The dark cloud had passed. By responding in a manner that communicated respect, by revealing something of my own vulnerability, and by doing all of that without necessarily appearing weak, I was able to defuse the intensity of the moment.

We all went on to have a productive day together. In the end, my detractor turned out to be one of the most enthusiastic of all the participants . . .

Afterwards, I retreat into the bathroom to catch a few moments of solitude. As I re-enter the conference room, I startle momentarily when I find HIM standing directly in my path. When he sees me, he smiles easily, his eyes radiant with transparent sincerity. He walks over, extending his hand, and says simply, "Thank you."

There can be no communion without transparency. So long as you hide who you are, you will always fail to connect with your audience (not to mention your work). Instead of worrying about being rejected, worry instead about whether your defenses are making you and your work inaccessible.

······ · ··●

More than a talent or skill, creativity reveals your essence to the world through your work. The most powerful creators open their souls, stand naked before us, willing to risk everything for a performance. Yes, you have apprehension, distrust, and doubt about stepping out. Yes, some rude people out there won't like you, but you can't let that worry hold you back. Take time to refocus. Recall the heart-strength that has gotten you this far and allow it to cradle your doubt. Ultimately, who you are is not only your fear; you are also that spark of light. Allow it to shine through.

Further Reflections On Transparency

To be a creator is to become *visible*. And to be visible you need to become *vulnerable*. If you wish to go deeper, explore one or more of the following questions. *Write, draw, dance, paint, meditate . . .*

☞ In what areas of my life do I fear showing my vulnerability to others? What might happen if people see me for who I am?

☞ Can I admit when I am wrong? How well do I tolerate criticism?

☞ In what ways do I hide from the world or from my creativity?

☞ What needs do I satisfy by keeping myself emotionally unavailable? At what point do I risk the vulnerability of being seen?

☞ In what ways do I share myself with others?

☞ What happened the last time I tried to be real with someone? What touched me? What frustrated me? What did I learn?

☞ What does my creative work reveal about me?

*Only a person who has a confident place to stand
internally can survive wearying periods of rejection
and censure . . .*

—Eric Maisel

*I want to know if you are prepared to live in the world
with its harsh need to change you. If you can look
back with firm eyes saying this is where I stand.*

—David Whyte

Make good thy standing place, and move the world.

—Goethe

Standing Place

ON A CREATIVE JOURNEY, we eventually reach a point where we must
stand alone. We can't necessarily count on others to usher us past
the many thresholds that must be crossed in the process of birthing
our ideas. Even when we do find people who take an interest in our
work, they may not always have our best interests at heart or understand our vision. If we want to step out and negotiate a place for
ourselves in the marketplace, we must first find a place to stand *inside*
ourselves.

If you recall from the section on Compassion, my original publisher
and I had an unexpected parting of the ways. For months after this
reversal of fortune, I wake up every day feeling adrift in a cold, wide
sea. I struggle to keep writing without any certainty that my efforts
will ever find an audience. With the memory of my humiliation so fresh,

I want to stop. But damn it, something inside me won't let me. I feel like I'm trudging through mud, but I persist anyway. Eight months later, I have the better part of a first draft completed. I mail an outline and some sample chapters to other small publishers and a few agents.

Some send me complimentary rejection letters ("Your thoughtful book shows promise, but it's just not what *we're* looking for right now, but this might be perfect for . . ."). Others express conditional interest. One publisher wants me to make changes that he assures me will make *Wild Ideas* "commercially viable." A particularly tempting offer comes from a New York agent who says she can sell *Wild Ideas* as a small "point of purchase" book provided I cut it by half: "Luv. Luv.Luv.Yur Contents," she says in a rhythm of brisk impatience.

I seriously consider this well-intentioned advice because, let's face it, I feel desperate to get my book published. Like an alcoholic in search of a drink to wash away a lingering hangover, I crave a publisher's acceptance as the only antidote to the bitter aftertaste of rejection. But none of it feels right. In each case, I feel I am betraying the book I aspire to write, not to mention the audience I hope to inspire.

What everyone advises seems so compelling. But my body rebels. Instead of feeling clear and focused after consultations with market-place experts, I experience the opposite—I feel more bewildered than ever. My stomach does flip-flops; my head swirls. I know only this: I refuse to strip the book of my voice, no matter who says they can sell it.

This is my standing place.

······•

"Make good thy standing place" was my father's oft-repeated admonition. Of all the teachings he strove to impart to his children, this one idea has had the greatest impact on my consciousness and has inspired much of my struggle for independence and self-realization.

My Father's words have **weight.**

*My Father's words buttress me again and again during dark times, bleak times, lonely times . . . so many times when I am beyond consolation. My father's words find me; hold me, uplift me—even against my will—*STAND UP.

······˙··●

When you have invested a lot of yourself in your creative work, you may find yourself emotionally unraveling when a promising opportunity doesn't work out as expected. You will almost always meet with a certain amount of indifference, rejection, or criticism once you venture forth bearing your gifts. A sensitive creator can, all too easily, take it much too much to heart: *If they aren't interested, if they don't like it, there must be something really wrong with my work . . . or, with me.*

We cannot control these kinds of thoughts or feelings. But we can, we must, recognize the intoxicating allure of playing the victim, and learn to manage our wounded pride more artfully.

Standing place provides a point of internal stability, both a ground of being and a "refuge of knowingness."

> *Knowing who I am.*
> *Knowing that I matter.*
> *Knowing what matters.*
> *Knowing I have enough of what it takes.*
> *Knowing my bottom line: what I will and won't do.*

When we feel most discouraged, the emotional resilience and internal clarity that characterize a standing place help us focus: *Who am I? What do I want to achieve?* Drawing from this inner strength, we find the love, energy, and commitment to give and give, and give some more, on behalf of what matters most. As inevitable setbacks occur, our standing

place supports us securely: we recover, we learn, we regroup, we step
out and try again.

·····$\cdot$··●

Unless, of course, you are convinced it is time to cut your losses, let
go, and move on.

Deep down, I know what I need: I need to partner with people I
can trust, who can see, and help shape, the potential for *Wild Ideas*,
without stripping it of its soul. But I can't seem to make it happen and
I can't attract what I need to me either. I keep walking into publishing
walls. A whirl of frenzy envelopes me. I feel more and more lost and
out of sync with the rhythms of the Universe.

Meanwhile, *other* opportunities for using my creativity beckon. I
take the not-so-subtle hint from the Universe: I decide to free up my
energy for something new and, frankly, something I can control.

The morning I finally let go, my heart forms a tight knot at the back
of my throat . . .

*I clear my desk, carefully laying well-worn pages of handwritten notes
and a hard copy of my manuscript inside a felt-lined box. My hands tremble
as I stand on tiptoe, placing the box into the farthest reaches of my closet,
back behind the jeans I only wear when I forget to do laundry. Sadness and
guilt wash over me. I think, "Someday." But deep down I know, someday may
never come. It feels like I am burying my stillborn child.*

·····$\cdot$··●

Timing is everything in business and, especially, in business that
matters to the heart.

•*a door closes*• *A Door Opens*

My passions and ambitions relocate themselves.

I feel myself drawn in a new direction. Forward into life. Into the modern-day gold rush that eventually becomes the real estate boom of the century. I leap at the opportunity to buy my first house. I ride the once-in-a-lifetime wave at dizzying speed until I get off, just in the nick of time—*before* it crashes on the shores of a bankrupt nation. Through it all, I paint, polish, plant—and flip. I treat each house as a canvas for my personal vision. During this time, I also reinvent my private practice, turning the next decade into the most satisfying years of my working life. I keep writing, expanding my quarterly missives into a monthly column that runs in a number of local papers. I begin painting again.

These are things I can do, things I can control—and, most importantly, things that nourish and strengthen my standing place.

Meanwhile . . .

Wild Ideas slumbers inside a box for the next twelve years.

In my early sixties, on the verge of retirement, after weathering the Great Recession, the death of my father, and a bout of chronic back pain, I experience the creeping realization that more days lie behind me than ahead of me. I have reached the stage of life when mortality becomes palpable. My thoughts turn to the time I have remaining on this earth. I ask myself: *What will I regret not having done?*

This question helps me rediscover my unfulfilled longing to leave a legacy of wisdom for those who come after me. In the weeks that follow, I dust off the box holding my precious opus. I begin reading the pages with fresh eyes; I feel a slight tug of desire but wince at the memory of what I may have to put myself through. Can I face it all again? *Do I have enough inside me?*

Weeks later, I run into an old friend at a Christmas party. When he asks what I'm up to I tell him about my long lost inspiration. "You have a book?" he asks incredulously. "I'd like to read it."

When he calls just one week after receiving the pages, he insists it needs to be published—and, miraculously, offers to help me.

In transition himself, my friend has been searching for a new project. He has impressive credentials as a former political operative and successful campaign manager and as the writer of three published books. Most importantly, he has a sincere, soulful character and understands what *Wild Ideas* can become. He boldly suggests that we start our own publishing company.

Reeling from this unexpected turn of events, I feel an initial flash of expectant terror, but my standing place recognizes the unmistakable knock of the Universe at my door. I have found the partner that I longed for—hiding in plain sight.

Timing is, indeed, everything. The time is finally right to take *Wild Ideas* to the marketplace.

······⋅··●

To survive in the world where creativity and business intersect, creators need the internal security that comes from having a place to stand. The global reach of the Internet has empowered more and more creators to take control of the business side of their lives and do-it-themselves.

But for those of you who want to partner with marketplace players, I offer this hard-won insight from my experience with people who control access to venues for public exposure such as galleries, theaters, or the media: *What people in positions of authority really need from you is assurance.* Sometimes the toughness and insensitivity that pass for power actually mask insecurity—a lack of a standing place. That's why you need to remain conscious of what is friendly, consistent, and wise inside yourself. *Your* standing place will keep you grounded in your values and objectives. Fortified with self-confidence, you can then present yourself and your work clearly and concisely.

Without the internal compass of a standing place, we may become lost. If we wish to preserve the emotional transparency that permits us to live as sensitive, imaginative, and connected creators, we must rely on the strength of standing place to support us from within. Standing place secures our ability to regenerate and reaffirm our internal resilience so we can risk the harshness, frustrations, fickleness, and reversals of the marketplace again and again, feel the intensity of what there is to feel, and return to ourselves intact.

Further Reflections On Standing Place

Claim your inner authority and set yourself free. If you wish to go deeper, explore one or more of the following questions. *Write, draw, dance, paint, meditate . . .*

☞ Am I ready to take ownership of my artistry? Do I trust my instincts? Are my priorities clear?

☞ What feelings arise as I get ready to step out and do business?

☞ How will I present myself and my work? (Hint: enthusiastically.) Who will benefit from my work? What background, credentials, or experience do I bring?

☞ What is my plan for reaching people who love what I do?

☞ Who do I know who can help me reach an audience? Who do I need to get to know? What people skills do I need to develop?

☞ Can I face criticism, make course corrections, and still find reasons to remain optimistic? In what ways can I draw strength from within myself?

☞ In what ways do I give away my power? Who am I afraid of disappointing or angering?

☞ What internal barriers prevent me from stepping out to promote myself and my work? Might I benefit from professional counseling, coaching, or mentoring? What local support groups exist for creators in my field?

☞ What is the best possible outcome? What might I have to sacrifice to realize my creative ambition?

☞ What is clear and constant at the core of my being, and how can it find expression?

Fame is a vapor, popularity an accident,
and riches take wings . . .

—Horace Greeley

If success is not on your own terms, if it looks
good to the world but does not feel good in your
heart, it is not success at all.

—Anna Quindlen

Failure is not the opposite of success,
it's part of success.

—Arianna Huffington

Success

A FRIEND OF MINE has just had his novel published and already has what most of us would consider the good fortune of getting a contract for another book. Instead of feeling ecstatic, as we might imagine we would feel in similar circumstances, he feels burdened by the incredible pressure to make it as good as the first. "It's not that I don't appreciate how lucky I am," he acknowledged, "but I feel like I'm going a little crazy."

I don't know about you, but I certainly wouldn't mind trading my current creative frustrations for the problems that come with that kind of success.

Let's face it, most creators yearn for success and acceptance from the outside world. Our longing makes us vulnerable to defining ourselves by standards that may not be suitable for living the life of an engaged creator whose values and priorities diverge from the norm. Creators who possess a healthy sense of self-preservation might ask themselves this question: *What does success mean to me? Is it an outward achievement that can be quantified, or is it an internal feeling? Or is it some of each?*

If you can't define success now, how will you know whether you have obtained it? Will you measure your success by how much money, prestige, and influence your work garners? Or will you feel successful because your creative work affords you a life that is fulfilled, challenged, and involved, even though you have to take a second job to make ends meet?

······˙··●

Don't get me wrong, turning your hard work and talent into gold can change your life in a number of positive ways. There's nothing quite like money to enable a lifestyle upgrade. You can finally quit that workaday job and become a full-time creator, invest in state-of-the-art equipment, or build a real studio in the back of the house. With enough money, you can even hire help. A house cleaner, a babysitter, or a production assistant can free you to focus on work or let you get some much needed rest. In addition, tremendous possibilities come along when your work finds popular appeal. Besides more challenging and interesting projects, you may discover opportunities to collaborate with other creators whom you have admired for years.

And then there's the satisfaction. After having labored at your craft for decades, it's difficult to beat the tremendous feeling of validation that accompanies hard-won recognition. It feels like a redemption for all those years of struggle.

On the other hand, the demands and pace of maintaining success frequently create just as many problems as they solve. Yes, you have more work for which you get handsomely paid, but you also have more obligations competing for your time and attention, leaving you with less time to work. I once heard an interview with Amy Tan in which the best-selling author complained that she had only one month of free time in which to write because she was so busy traveling and speaking about her books—as opposed to actually writing them. In our hunger for success, we need to recognize that along with the rewards comes a whole new level of responsibility, pressure, and tension that can complicate the challenges inherent to the process of creation.

······˙··●

The creature comforts and other tangible rewards of success promise to make us happier, but they often don't. As a young child, I grew up in a modest neighborhood, located on the fringes of conspicuous wealth. I spent much of my childhood wishing our family could move up from our small, cracker-box house in the flats into the hills of the affluent suburb nearby. I just knew, in the innocent way a small child believes in the magic of fairy tales, that all our secret shames could be redeemed if only we lived in a bigger, brighter house.

When I was fifteen, we finally made the move I had dreamed about for so long. But the rebirth I sought at the top of the hill continued to elude me. Whatever else might have changed, my family's upscale surroundings failed to help me feel any less of an outsider. Looking back, I learned an invaluable lesson about the limitations of material success as compensation for feelings of deprivation or inadequacy.

Not long after that move, I made another. This time I ensconced myself in the counterculture of the UC Berkeley campus, where I discovered a new generation of idealistic young people challenging the American mania for high-profile achievement. The books I devoured on philosophy and spirituality offered a broader and deeper definition of success.

As I write this, I recall Carlos Castaneda's magical tale of sorcery and mystical knowledge, *The Teachings of Don Juan*. In it, the central character Don Juan explains to his young protégé that although all paths are the same in that they eventually "lead nowhere," the most joyful journey can be found on "the path with heart." I decided then that if I could travel my heart-path, I would consider my life a success.

······ˑ··●

Flash forward to the present. We hear a lot these days about *following the path with heart*. In many ways, society grants much more latitude than ever before for living a creative, idiosyncratic life. As a culture, we applaud successful entrepreneurs who reinvent the rules of the game. But we also live in a paradoxical time. It seems as if the widespread popularity of social media has actually increased the pressures to fit in—to look a certain way, speak a certain way, act a certain way. Listening to the quiet murmurs of the heart doesn't come easily when we are assailed by a constant barrage of sound bites and images competing for our time and attention.

Successfully navigating the path with heart requires us to overcome our relentless self-judgments—and stop comparing our lives with the lives of others. Letting go of self-judgement can be especially difficult because of our conflicting needs. As creators, we want to *achieve* something special and unique. As human beings, we want to *belong*. Finding a way of *belonging to ourselves* and a way of *belonging to the world* becomes one important measure of success.

As much as I pride myself on being my own person, a small part of me longs for the kind of high-profile success I turned away from when I was young. I still do get very, very excited when it looks like I might be on the verge of making it in a BIG way. There have been some stellar moments: I was positively thrilled when a state senator and a television newscaster each bought one of my paintings. What creator doesn't enjoy receiving validation from important people? But the earth didn't move, the seas didn't part, and the heavens didn't open. The very next day, I was back drawing in the kitchen of my five-room cottage, trying to figure out what shade of green to use. And even though I appeared on a PBS television series, I never did hear from Oprah.

·······•

Unfortunately, few creators receive the public recognition and material rewards they perhaps deserve. If your natural inclinations, talents, and temperament leave you no other option than to follow your passions down an uncertain road, then it becomes vital that you set reasonable, life-affirming standards for achievement. Otherwise, the longing for success and its attendant rewards can become a constant, unquenchable thirst—an overwhelming need that will eventually come between you and your work, souring your relationship to life.

I have a friend who has been writing all his life. Nearly sixty years old, he has done odd and interesting jobs to support himself while his wife works as a teacher. He has written for newspapers and published articles in magazines. Most importantly, he writes novels and has self-published a number of them. Through dogged determination, he has sold thousands of copies and managed to make back his investment of capital plus a little extra. He gets fan mail from readers and is a local celebrity of sorts. But even with the help of agents, my friend has not been able to get a publisher interested in his work. When I spoke to him a few weeks ago, I could hear in his voice how deeply disheartened and bitter he has become and it made me feel sad. He has dedicated himself to his talent. His writing is funny and crisp and he has managed to do what very few people have. He has kept on writing despite a lack of commercial success.

·····.····●

There are two kinds of failure. In the first, we do our best and it turns out to be not good enough to reach a specific objective—like coming in fourth at the Olympics after having trained for the gold. Such a situational failure, although tremendously disappointing, brings no dishonor if we have put our heart and soul into the attempt. The capacity to be fully invested in the service of a dream is an achievement in itself and speaks to a triumph of character that eclipses the outcome.

In the second kind, we fail to transcend our own self-destructive impulses. When we allow our damaged places to tear us down or hold us back, we become our own worst enemy. When we permit disappointment and frustration to sink bitter roots into the heart, we engender enmity. Bitterness corrodes the soul because it robs us of love. Just when we need love most, it's least available to us.

We must come to value the validity of our struggles as creators. There is success and even nobility in struggle. Success in and of itself has little worth unless we can discover some deeper meaning within its achievement. Likewise, with the right attitude, even failure can be an important source of inspiration. As the author William Saroyan wrote, "Good people are good because they've come to wisdom through failure." Material success matters, but unless it embraces an opening of the heart, its achievement will eventually ring hollow.

Further Reflections On Success

Creative success depends on syncing your heart's desire to the power of your will. If you wish to go deeper, explore one or more of the following questions. *Write, draw, dance, paint, meditate . . .*

☞ What do I think about when I imagine success? (Public acclaim? Feeling challenged? Personal growth? Making a difference? Doing what I love? Pressure and responsibility? Making money? Deriving meaning from what I do? Taking care of my family? Something else?)

☞ Do professional *opportunities* feel more like *obligations* rather than exciting adventures? What goals for success would be a better fit for who I really am?

☞ How do my daily habits support my ability to succeed? (What are some ways I can set boundaries to protect my time, resources, and talents? Do my choices support physical and mental health? Do I surround myself with supportive people?)

☞ Is my desire sufficiently strong to overcome my fears? What specific fears will I need to address?

☞ How can I tolerate setbacks and come back stronger? What do I need to keep myself going?

☞ When a situation doesn't work out, can I feel successful because I have developed new skills, friendships, and connections?

☞ To what extent am I willing to work hard and sacrifice? What work-play-life balance and level of success will make me happiest?

☞ What markers all along the way show me whether or not I am succeeding?

☞ What holds me back from achieving the level of success that I want? (Are my expectations too high or too low? Do I avoid taking necessary risks? Do I fear failure? Am I unwilling or unable to change?)

☞ In what ways do I keep myself from feeling successful because I am too hard on myself?

☞ How do my old failures still hold me captive? Can I let go of that old idea and allow myself to be something else—something new— in the future?

☞ To what extent do I base my worth as a person solely on the magnitude of my achievements?

☞ Does the pursuit of success leave me feeling energized or depleted? What new choices will restore more balance in my life?

☞ If success is also a matter of personal growth or character, what personal challenges have I been able to overcome?

☞ Consider author Bertha Damon: "Getting what you go after is *success*; but liking it while you are getting it is *happiness*."

*In giving thanks, we become open to dimensions
beyond the purely personal.*

—Gordon Onslow Ford

*The essence of all beautiful art, all great art,
is gratitude.*

—Frederick Nietzsche

*Though a tree grows ever higher, the falling leaves
return to the ground.*

—Malay proverb

Gratitude

AS MUCH AS WE MAY PRIDE OURSELVES on our fierce independence and
self-reliance, all of us receive help along the way. We frequently receive
support from friends and family who tolerate erratic moods and
demanding schedules, all the while offering encouragement. We also
owe much to the marketplace decision makers who make it possible
for our work to be seen by a wider audience, which, if we are fortunate, displays its appreciation by purchasing our work. With a grateful
heart, we thank those people and energies, both seen and unseen, that
have affected the course of our creative lives.

When I first began sending my thoughts and feelings out into the
world, I waited in nervous wonderment. How would my offerings be
received? And when those first, mostly positive, responses trickled
in, I felt every note, every call, every kind word, as a warm embrace.

I felt profoundly grateful for every bit of encouragement shepherding me past my apprehensions. And that encouragement empowered me to step out again.

Time after time, just when I've been ready to give up, just when my spirits have been at their lowest, just when I've most needed reassurance that what I do matters, someone has sent a small gift of appreciation in gratitude for something I have written. I have always interpreted such coincidences of timing as signs from the Universe to stay the course.

Like many creators, I am insecure by nature. When the doom and gloomy side of myself takes hold, navigating the creative process becomes even more challenging. During those periods, gratitude does not come easily. Yet along with the considerable baggage of cynicism, something else inside me finds reasons to keep creating and sharing my gifts with others. Despite occasions when everything appears dark and hopeless, that spacious spirit keeps looking for ways to turn me into an optimist. Whatever hope I have been able to sustain has been due to the part of me that retains faith in the goodness of people and the fundamental generosity of the Universe.

Gratitude grants us the possibility of discovering wholeheartedness amidst life's disappointments. Whenever our *inner cynic* is in charge, we take for granted, dismiss, or overlook entirely those small acts of acknowledgement that come our way. When we feel resentful or undeserving, when we dwell in emotional negativity, we become blind to the potential value of our work. Without some measure of optimism, some smidgen of gratitude to sustain us, we may not find the courage to step out with our creations.

······ꞏ··●

It has been my experience that once you have made a commitment to creative work—and provided it is a good fit with who you are—the

Universe will send you messages of encouragement and support in unexpected ways. I recall how early on, when the notion of writing a book was completely beyond my comprehension, a friend gathered together a collection of my writings and bound them into a beautiful handmade volume. Her quiet gesture was more than a thoughtful gift. Seeing the cumulative weight of my collected writings offered me tangible proof that a book was within my capabilities.

I am always stunned by the ubiquity and immensity of simple human kindness and the sheer unexpectedness of it. Throughout my journey there have been so many people who have extended themselves at precisely the right moment, and that has made all the difference.

Ironically, as devastated as I was at the time, I am now eternally grateful to my original publisher for backing out of our agreement. Her initial interest and enthusiasm helped make this book possible; her subsequent rejection strengthened my determination to succeed and freed me to follow my own vision.

People who have disappointed us—and even people we have never met—contribute to our journey in small but important ways. Whether every specific offer of assistance ultimately leads to a tangible result is beside the point. We can be grateful for the intangible rays of encouragement, like beacons of hope, guiding us towards the possibility of success.

······⋅··●

We must be mindful of a larger gratitude as well—we can be thankful for creativity itself. Many of us have been sustained through periods of great difficulty because we could turn to creative work for solace and companionship. For the past thirty years, writing and painting have been devotional practices, not vocational paths. They allow me to offer up my fear, hope, wisdom, loneliness, and disappointment. I can count on the creative process to comfort and enlighten me if I make the effort to engage. I am intensely grateful for its reassuring presence, like a friend who accepts me for whatever I am.

Some creators believe that during periods of deep concentration and consuming engagement, we tap into something beyond personal consciousness. In the process of penetrating our own mind and heart, we eventually encounter the deepest layer of knowing that the psychologist Carl Jung termed "the collective unconscious." Here we discover a timeless reservoir of shared human experience. As creators, we dip into this boundless well of inspiration and, in turn, pass the gift on to others in the form of works that beautify, inform, inspire, or serve the world.

We can be grateful for the opportunity to connect with the vastness of that quiet expanse, brimming over with untold riches of knowledge and wisdom. That we can go to this well whenever we like, as often as we like, is such a generous offering that it boggles the mind. Imagine: *a constant source of inspiration waiting to fill us, if only we will open ourselves to it.*

We cannot will creative expression through the power of the mind or personality. We can only prepare ourselves for the possibility of connection by maturing our skills and talents, coming out of hiding, and finding our way. If we can accept the idea that creativity is a gift, then we can give up trying to force it and instead simply embrace creativity as an ever-present potential in our lives.

Despite everything inside us that appears small, muddled, and afraid, we also contain a spirit that is large, clear, and infinite. Viewed from an inclusive perspective, we contain both possibility and impossibility, depending on where we look. Be grateful for the passionate creator inside you that wants to open your life to the wonder of new horizons.

Further Reflections On Gratitude

How does gratitude feed your creativity? If you wish to go deeper, explore one or more of the following questions. *Write, draw, dance, paint, meditate . . .*

☞ Can I take a moment to acknowledge the circumstances I am grateful for today? Hint: What made me happy? What inspired me? What brought me comfort or peace? What did I learn? What difficulty deepened my awareness? What barrier did I overcome?

☞ What opportunities, talents, or privileges have I been given? In what ways do these gifts empower me creatively?

☞ What kindness have I taken for granted in the past that I might appreciate today?

☞ Who are the people who have nurtured my creativity? How have they fed my progress? In what ways might I express my appreciation?

☞ How do my fears prevent me from experiencing gratitude for all the good in my life? How might lack of gratitude impact my ability to feel creatively inspired?

☞ Recalling the last time I expressed my appreciation, how did that make me feel? What happened to that sense of gratitude?

☞ In what way has a misfortune become an unforeseen blessing? What insights can I use from the experience to shed light on a current challenge?

➤ Having come all this way, how have I changed from the person I used to be? What have I achieved? What new appreciation of myself can I cultivate as a result?

➤ How can I show my gratitude by sharing my creativity with others?

➤ I want to enlarge my capacity for gratitude: What person in my life most needs my forgiveness?

➤ Consider Albert Schweitzer: "Sometimes our light goes out but is blown into flame by another human being. Each of us owes deepest thanks to those who have rekindled this light."

Trust the light that brought you to this place to keep guiding you on your journey.

—*Diane Frank*

The human mind is always making progress
but it is a progress of spirals.

—Madame de Staël

Progress has not followed a straight ascending
line, but a spiral with rhythms . . . of evolution
and dissolution.

—Goethe

I didn't know this then—or not
in the way that I know it now.

—Katherine Angel

Closing
the creative spiral

SPIRALS HAVE BEEN USED IN ART since primitive times. One of the oldest symbols of our endlessly evolving journey through life, the spiral has been found carved into cave dwellings, rocks, and tombs all over the world. Traditionally, the spiral has been associated with the cycles of birth, death, and rebirth as humanity rounds the rhythms of time, nature, and her seasons.

The spiral is an eternal journey.
The spiral is a healing journey.

More recently, the spiral metaphor has become synonymous with psychological growth and healing. The spiral reminds us of our potential for progress, despite those periods when it feels like we are going in circles. We are all familiar with the frustration of having made what appear to be new choices, only to discover the same old pitfalls lurking within them. Sooner or later, we find ourselves lamenting, "Oh, no. Not this again."

> *The spiral is a journey of return.*
> *The spiral is a journey of discovery.*

Provided we live our lives as conscious beings, these cycles do not have to become endless loops—that is the beauty of the spiral metaphor. There is always the possibility of learning, deepening, and ascending. Imagine the spiral as a three-dimensional staircase: Each time we come around and meet those familiar traps and tendencies, we have the chance to respond from a slightly different vantage point. For all our days, we walk the great spiral, traversing its curves, sometimes moving upwards, other times stumbling and falling backwards.

> *The spiral is a journey of progression and retrogression.*
> *The creative journey is a spiral.*

The creative process can also be viewed from the perspective of the spiral. While working on a project, creators progress through the various stages once, twice, sometimes many times, sometimes in one order, sometimes in another. Cycles of inspiration, discovery, creation, frustration, fulfillment, and emptiness help us mature as creators as well as human beings. Each time we pass through a stage, we integrate new information along with a deeper range of feelings; we learn new skills by taking advantage of more resources. Above all, we get better at nurturing ourselves. As we grow more conscious, we become more willing to make fundamental changes in our attitudes, habits, and priorities, which, in turn, empower us to produce better work. This is how we advance along the creative spiral.

•••••·•••●

The painter Paul Klee once wrote, "The art of mastering life is the prerequisite for all further forms of expression." Ultimately, whether we are carving a statue, composing a poem, or growing a business, the creative process is about the way we live our lives—especially the choices we make. That is why it is possible to be a successful creator without ever writing a word or painting a picture. Shaping our lives is our greatest creative work.

Each of us engages in a singular journey of exploration and revelation. We struggle to express our deepest truth just as working artists do. How do we find the courage to live what we love? Do we stay with what is safe and familiar, even though it feels deadened and false? Do we continue with habits of reactive behavior that undermine us and hurt the people we love? Or do we risk the pain of opening our minds and hearts in order to grow? At the most ordinary times our creativity can inspire us to find our way through difficult challenges in both our personal and professional lives.

The creative journey contains a myriad of pleasures as well as perils. When things get difficult, take a breath and remember these three important principles you can practice to encourage your own progress.

First, reclaim the outliers within your psyche. Your most important creative assets frequently turn out to be all that is tentative, flawed, outrageous, and out of step within you. Remember—your vulnerabilities can become *fertile limits,* dictating the direction and depth of your process, rather than impeding it.

Second, become more self-nurturing. Instead of forcing something into being, allow your creation to emerge in its own time.

Third, familiarize yourself with the stages of the creative process and, especially, with your particular style of navigating those stages.

By identifying where you are in the creative process, you will find it much easier to stay the course.

······•

If you have more questions after reading *Wild Ideas*, so much the better. Let your curiosity inspire further explorations. There is no one right answer or method. You might go back and review a section that resonates, or one that disturbs you. Create something in response or delve a little deeper into the reflections at the end of that section. Perhaps you wish to expand your knowledge and practical skills by seeking out additional reading, taking a workshop, or finding a mentor. Go ahead, unwrap that canvas. Open those tubes of paint that have been sitting on your shelf for six months. Make your mark. See what happens.

Wherever you are in your process, whatever dreams you are struggling to realize, *please, hang in there.* Keep listening to that small, stubborn voice loving you in secret, calling you to your truest life. You already know what to do at some level. Trust that knowing. Take the first step and the next. Look for allies—and know that I am one of them. I am rooting for you. May you continue to be nourished and challenged by your dreams.

It has been my deepest pleasure to have taken you through this journey of discovery and creative possibility. If you have found the ideas expressed here helpful, I'd love to hear from you. Please keep in touch through my website and blog at cathywild.com.

When it's over, I want to say: all my life
I was a bride married to amazement.

—*Mary Oliver*

Epilogue

AT THIS TIME OF YEAR, nature's vanity shows off her handiwork in a riot-
ous, eye-popping display of color. Outside my window, the valley echoes
with the sounds of celebration as another successful growing season
comes to an end. Meanwhile, I have a harvest of my own to celebrate.

In completing *Wild Ideas* more than a dozen years after I first con-
ceived it, I have finally kept a difficult promise. I have trusted when
it seemed more prudent not to, and persevered when it seemed I had
forgotten why I started. Sometimes the only thing that kept me going
was my vow to finish.

And I have learned things.

I have learned that letting go of a dream isn't the same as abandoning it.
Some dreams cycle around again and find you even when you aren't
looking for them. I have learned that I am tougher than I knew. I have
withstood a slow burning in allowing myself to be worn down at one
level so that my heart could reveal itself at another. I have learned that

I have what writer Michael Ventura calls "a talent for the room." My soul feels nourished by the solitary, often painful, process of simply sitting quietly in a chair and getting the job done. Hidden ecstasy can be found in the labor of fulfilling a promise.

Any accomplishment comes with a price.
The creative journey is a paradox.

To arrive at an ending is to discover an unsettling contradiction. Beyond the unquestionable delight, the sheer joy in accomplishing something that has felt beyond my capabilities, I have come home from my creative exertions feeling dislocated from familiar touchstones. Distances have opened in my absence without my consent. In growing beyond my former limits, aspects of life no longer satisfy; old connections fall away even as new ones form. Author and intrepid adventurer Cindy Ross once wrote that it can be difficult to return home after a long-distance journey because "you have grown outside the puzzle and your piece no longer fits."

It seems that I have arrived
At an unexpected path to what happens next.
I am shedding old, weathered skin.
I am transparent . . . tentative . . . new.

All that I love is leaving and washing over me at the same time.
And I have begun to cherish the loneliness of it.
And the simple, infinite promise.
I am shedding memories: shining and perishable.

I am new. I am old.
I am more and more myself.
So this is what enough *feels like . . .*
As good as a feast.

—Cathy Wild

Honor the space between no longer and not yet.

—*Nancy Levin*

Recognition

WILD IDEAS HAS BEEN MANY YEARS in the making. All along the way there have been so many people whose friendship, feedback, and enthusiasm for the project have supported my efforts. In particular, I wish to thank the early readers of the manuscript for their in-depth notes and thoughtful feedback: Katie Alvord, Joan Frank, Debbie Gray, Jill Nussinow, Steve Silverman, and Joel Crockett.

To Karen Rose and Roy Carlisle for seeing and believing.

Appreciation to my friends in the Sonoma County Dance Community for encouragement and companionship. And to new friends from the seaside community of Gualala, where I rewrote a large portion of the manuscript.

For countless kindnesses I wish to acknowledge Don and Carol Bickel, Linda Hunt, Nick Kishmirian, and especially R. A. Benson. Each of you helped me to keep the faith in one way or another.

For challenging critique of my writing thank you to Susan Bono, whose early edits toughened me up and taught me to appreciate the value of criticism. My everlasting gratitude goes to Ray Dean Mize, tireless advocate for the active verb. Thank you for dedicating so much of your personal time to editing these pages. Kudos to my copy editor Jane Mackay for helping me fine-tune the final version.

To my parents, June and Jerry, for providing the crucible events and life-shaping experiences that launched me on my journey of discovery. And especially to my indomitable Grandma Dora, who showed me the power of persistence each and every day.

Hugs of appreciation go to my sister, Lisa, for emotional and editorial support through all the long years and multiple versions of the manuscript. I love you.

My deepest gratitude goes to Guy Conner, whose belief in the book, unwavering support, and unfailing optimism have made the publication of *Wild Ideas* possible.

Finally, I would like to thank my clients, fellow travelers, for giving me the opportunity to share my gifts and for continuing to teach me that any journey taken with faith, love, and sincerity is and will always be something worth doing.

About the Author

CATHY WILD HAS SPENT more than thirty years developing innovative approaches to healing that integrate powerful body-centered techniques with the creative process. While expanding her private practice, Cathy became a popular speaker, workshop leader, and corporate consultant. She has facilitated women's groups, writing groups, and book groups; and has taught in the extended education program at Santa Rosa Junior College. As a pioneer in somatic counseling, the expressive arts, and the field of life coaching, Cathy was featured as a creativity expert on the PBS television series, *In the Prime*. Today, her life's work has deepened and evolved into Body-Centered Healing—a dynamic, experiential process that supports clients on a profound personal journey of transformation. When she isn't writing, you can find Cathy painting in the studio, puttering in the garden, or baking up a batch of cookies for her friends. Cathy lives in Northern California and online at cathywild.com.

FOR MORE INFORMATION

on private consultations and book orders

or to view artwork by Cathy Wild

visit www.cathywild.com

"You are going through labor pains right now — you are trying to birth something and it hurts to try to get it out. but keep pushing, keep breathing — there is joy in delivery, something beatiful to behold — you know what I keep saying — Come, Work, Play, Trust" —

Made in the USA
Columbia, SC
02 November 2019